Celtic All-Time Greats

Parkhead Legends

Celtic

All-Time Greats

*Parkhead
Legends*

Above: Four of Jock Stein's
famous Lisbon Lions – John Clark,
Jimmy Johnstone, Billy McNeill
and Steve Chalmers.

Parragon
13 Whiteladies Road
Clifton
Bristol BS8 1PB

Reprinted 1998

ISBN 0-75252-671-5

This independent
publication has been
prepared without any
involvement on the part of
Celtic Football Club or
The Scottish FA.

Contents

Introduction

Glasgow, they say, is no mean city – and in the course of the century that's passed since their formation back in 1888, Celtic have proved that they are no mean football team. Their history had already been long and glorious when Jock Stein, a former player of note, returned to Paradise (as the ground has always been colloquially known) to take charge in 1965.

Under the authoritative eye of the Big Man, the club swiftly transcended its Scottish origins to become an acknowledged power on the global scene, becoming the first British club to bring the European Cup to these shores. What is more, the League win that proved their passport to glory was just one of nine in a row, from 1966 to 1974, that set a Scottish record that's only recently been rivalled.

The origins of the club among the Irish immigrant population of Glasgow may have been seized upon by others in the light of sectarian strife in Ireland, but it's a proud legacy Celtic have never tried to hide. And while they've boasted in their ranks Eire internationals like Packy Bonner, 80 times capped by his country, the playing staff in recent years has become more cosmopolitan than ever.

That said, the famed Lisbon Lions who took European club football's ultimate prize in 1967 – beating the fabled Inter Milan – nearly all came from within a 30-mile radius of Glasgow. Their willingness to work tirelessly for each other, combined with the defence-splitting skills of flying winger Jimmy Johnstone, proved too potent a combination for the Italians, and the Scottish League proved equally powerless to resist.

Below: Excellence has always been Celtic's aim – and Jorge Cadete, who registered 30 goals in 37 League appearances during his first two campaigns at Parkhead, was acquired from Sporting Lisbon with this in mind.

A new wave of talent came through in the 1970s, which suggested the glories of past years would be maintained. But one by one, the likes of Dalglish and Macari went on to make bigger names for themselves south of the border, where the rewards were greater than in Glasgow. The pattern would be repeated in the 1980s with Charlie Nicholas among those to join the talent drain. In the 1990s, of course, the Bosman ruling has let the likes of John Collins decamp to Monaco without the club receiving any recompense whatsoever.

The exception that proved the rule came in the shape of Paul McStay, club captain and long-time midfielder whose retirement in the summer of 1997 ended an era. He was cast from the same mould as the likes of Jimmy McGrory, the record goalscorer who was so dedicated to the hoops that he simply refused to consider a transfer to Arsenal, and Billy McNeill, the towering defender around whom Stein built his team and who would manage the club in two separate spells. These men knew the meaning of loyalty and fans returned that one thousandfold in their devotion.

Above: Lou Macari, Harry Hood and Bobby Lennox in action against Rangers during the 1971 Scottish Cup Final replay which Celtic won 2-1.

ITALIAN STYLE

Glasgow football 1990s-style is a colourful, cosmopolitan affair, even if the major players aren't necessarily there for the duration. The recruitment of Italian wing wizard Paolo Di Canio to join the volatile but immensely creative Jorge Cadete in the course of the 1996-97 season, not only made Celtic the most pleasurable team to watch in the Scottish League – it also enriched the Scots scene as a whole, as was proved when Di Canio ran off with the Player of the Year award. Glasgow is no longer a footballing arena for Glaswegians alone, if indeed it ever was.

And with this influx of 'foreign' talent has come the attention of the world's press. This, in turn, has brought even more intense pressures – a demand for instant success that has reduced the 'life expectancy' of managers to a matter of a few seasons at most. Sadly, Celtic have suffered more than their fair share

of the 'revolving door' policy in recent years, the last victim being playing favourite Tommy Burns. His departure was a shock to many who felt he was on the brink of turning things around, but he was not to have the time or the opportunity to complete the job. With Celtic's deadly rivals firmly in the ascendant, nothing better than first place would do.

DUTCH COURAGE

Now, with coach Wim Jansen (who, incidentally, played for Feyenoord when they beat Celtic in the 1970 European Cup Final) in harness with general manager Jock Brown, they could well be back in the hunt for honours. Former player and one-time manager David Hay was appointed chief scout and immediately made his presence felt by recommending the purchase of Hibs' Darren Jackson – the first brick in the new management team's rebuilding policy. Former Lisbon Lion John Clark was also invited back on the staff as kit manager.

So it is to this mixture of old and new faces that Celtic have looked in their bid to bring the big time back to Parkhead. This book outlines some of the names that made Celtic the legend they are today – if Brown and Jansen's plans should come to fruition, there's plenty of scope for a second volume.

Glasgow Celtic Club History

When Celtic triumphed in Lisbon in 1967's European Cup Final, they wrote an unforgettable climax to a story that had begun nearly a century earlier with the formation of Celtic Football and Athletic Club. The intention then had been to form a charitable organisation to raise money for the poor of Glasgow's East End, the vision behind it being the leader of a local teaching institute named Brother Walfrid.

The name on everyone's lips in 1967, though, was that of the great Jock Stein, a man who'd led the Celts on the pitch and returned to guide them to the biggest prize in club football. A far cry from those lowly beginnings, but a foundation for future glories that would include nine League Championships in a row (1966-74). It's those heights the club seeks to regain as the 20th Century ends and we enter a new millenium.

Brother Walfrid, for his part, had rather less grandiose ambitions in mind back in 1888. In addition to charitable ventures, he wanted to provide the Irish population with a club to call their own. Scotland already had one such team, Hibernian in Edinburgh, which, until the clause was dropped in 1893, had been committed to sign only Catholics. Many of Celtic's players were poached from the Edinburgh team, who ironically had been one of the sides on view (along with Cowlairs) when Celtic Park was opened in May 1888.

SCOTTISH RIVALRY

The main rivals-to-be, however, came from rather closer at hand. Glasgow Rangers had history on their side, having been formed in 1873, and the two teams locked horns in Celtic's very first friendly match. Pre-kick-off odds

WILLS'S CIGARETTES

J. DELANEY (CELTIC)

J. McGRORY.

Left: The legendary Jimmy McGrory served Celtic from 1921 to 1965, firstly as a player and then as manager.

Above: Jimmy Delaney, a Parkhead star of the 1930s before his transfer to Manchester United.

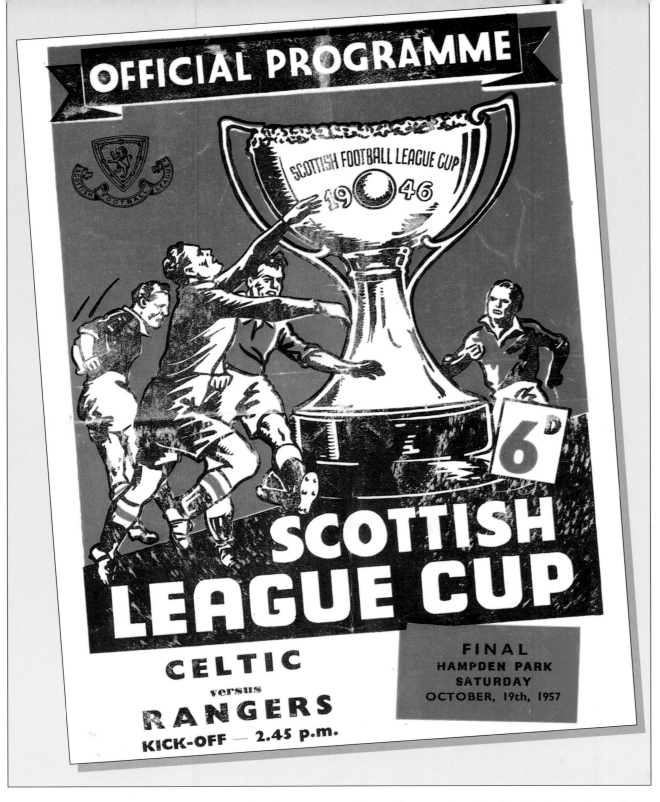

OFFICIAL PROGRAMME

SCOTTISH FOOTBALL LEAGUE CUP
1946

6D

SCOTTISH LEAGUE CUP

CELTIC
versus
RANGERS
KICK-OFF — 2.45 p.m.

FINAL
HAMPDEN PARK
SATURDAY
OCTOBER, 19th, 1957

Above left: Matches between Glasgow's two premier clubs were always guaranteed to make headlines. Their 1957 League Cup Final meeting, which ended 7-1 to Celtic, was certainly no exception.

favoured the established team, but it was the side in green that ran out 5-2 winners. The reported crowd was some 2,000 strong, women being admitted free while others paid sixpence a head. Yet the most fascinating fact must surely be that the two sets of players chose to wind down together by sharing tea (and, apparently, indulging in a spot of community singing) in a local hall. Hardly the image of the fixture in more recent years…

The Scottish League opened for business in 1890-91 and Celtic were keen competitors from the outset, despite losing their first game 4-1 to the now-defunct Renton. They made steady progress, rising from third through second to Champions in successive seasons and retaining their title in 1893-94. September 1898's meeting with Rangers at Parkhead (who themselves had finished Champions that season) brought a crowd of 44,868, underlining the fact that the rivalry was already highly profitable in terms of bodies through the turnstiles.

It was clear, too, that the old order, in the shape of the once-dominant and strictly amateur side Queen's Park, was about to change in the face of the dual domination from the blue and green. They hadn't even entered the Scottish League until 1900-01, considering it both a threat to the Cup and amateur status, and to this day have never finished higher than fifth in the table.

As in England, where celebrated amateur outfits like Wanderers and Old Carthusians had been swept aside by the new professionalism, so the advent of the League had taken Scottish football into a new dimension. Celtic administrator John McLaughlin, who served as the League's first secretary, was an unrepentant believer in the new order and likened attempts to stem the tide of professionalism to 'attempting to stop the flow of Niagara with a kitchen chair'. Brother Walfrid and his charitable aims had long since been overtaken by events and Celtic became a limited company in 1897, five years after he'd

9

Above: Nine titles in a row plus the European Cup made the managerial reputation of 'Big Man' Jock Stein well nigh unassailable.

departed Glasgow for a position in England. They continued, however, their strong association with the Irish-Catholic community.

If Rangers had been in the ascendant at the turn of the century, with four League titles on the trot, the first decade of the new century undeniably belonged to Celtic, who snapped up six successive Championships between 1904-10.

This was achieved under the leadership of Willie Maley, the club's first secretary-manager, who'd been appointed in April 1897 just after the club became a limited company. The four-trophy season of 1907-08 marked the first time any club had held League, Cup, Glasgow and Charity Cups simultaneously.

There could well have been a hat-trick of 'Doubles' also had it not been for the match of 1909 where only Rangers stood in the way of a third such feat. The first game ended in a 2-2 draw, the second 1-1 – but the Scottish FA withheld the Cup due to disgraceful scenes after 90 minutes. The 'Hampden Riot' wrote a sorry page in the history books. Both clubs were ordered to compensate hosts Queen's Park for the damage caused by their so-called fans.

Football north of the border continued through the First World War, though the Scottish Cup was suspended

and players' wages reduced to £2 a week. Celtic very nearly made it through the period as undisputed Champs. Somehow, it was Rangers who took their crown by a single point – but Celtic's 62-match unbeaten record was undeniably impressive.

CUP CHEER

Celtic regained the title in 1918-19, and won four more titles in the period between the wars. In fact, the Glasgow stranglehold was such that through the 1920s the pennant never left the city. The 1924-25 season saw Celtic's name on the Cup – beating their Rangers rivals by five goals to nil *en route*. Two of those goals were scored by the legendary Jimmy McGrory, who notched in every round and would go on to manage the club after the legendary Willie Maley. This, their 11th victory in the Scottish Cup, gave them the lead over previous record holders Queen's Park.

The inter-war years saw the name of McStay appear in the team sheet for the first time. Willie and Jimmy McStay were the great-great-uncles of future superstar Paul, while other players of note included John Thomson, the Scottish international goalkeeper who'd die tragically and accidentally in 1931 at the feet of Rangers centre-forward Sam English.

Jimmy McGrory retired in 1937, but not before he'd taken part in a Scottish Cup Final, played against Aberdeen, which attracted a crowd of 146,433 – a record between two British clubs which still stands to this very day. Also of note was an eight-team tournament staged to celebrate the Empire Exhibition of 1938, which saw Celtic face Sunderland and Everton. A late Johnny Crum goal brought the Celts the honours.

On the managerial front, 71-year-old Willie Maley was replaced by Jimmy McStay and then another former player, Jimmy McGrory, who thus became Celtic's third manager in their history. But the postwar years saw little success at Parkhead, especially after folk hero Jimmy Delaney's departure to Manchester United after well over a decade's service in peace and war.

The arrival of defender Jock Stein (from Welsh non-League side Llanelli Town) as captain in 1951 boosted Celtic's fortunes and they followed the winning of the Scottish Cup (their first trophy of note in 13 years, achieved prior to Stein's appearance) with the League and Cup Double three years later. Stein, of course, had another pivotal role to play and when appointed manager, in 1965, he became just the fourth person to have occupied the Parkhead hotseat.

His arrival was not before time. Aside from the League Cup Final of October 1957 – which Celtic won by a 7-1 margin – little had shaken Rangers' continued stranglehold on the Scottish scene. Indeed, in the period from 1957 until Stein's arrival, Celtic would fail to pick up any of Scotland's three major trophies, while their rivals achieved four League titles plus an equal number of wins in both League and FA trophies.

A GOLDEN AGE

Jock Stein changed all that of course – and his return was to herald a golden age. From 1966 to 1974 inclusive, they turned in nine Championships in a row, establishing a dominance they've yet to repeat. They also reached the Scottish League and FA Cup Finals in three consecutive years, from 1965-67.

Below: Former Rangers fan Danny McGrain rewarded Celtic with over 650 appearances in all competitions between 1970-87 and was himself honoured with the MBE.

13

Right: Winger David Provan cost Celtic a six-figure fee in 1978, but a diagnosis of ME in 1986 effectively ended his career.

Below: Having left Parkhead in 1987 to try his luck in German football, Murdo MacLeod returned ten years later as assistant to new coach Wim Jansen.

But it was the Lisbon Lions, all bar one born within 30 miles of Parkhead, who were responsible for Celtic's finest hour. Had it not been for a late disallowed Lennox goal, they could have made the Final in Stein's first full season with the club. It was disallowed, apparently for being offside, and Liverpool won the day.

No such refereeing error could stop Celtic in 1967. 'The greatness of a club in modern football will be judged on performances in Europe,' Stein had said after Celtic had been crowned League Champions in 1966 – and the side backed his words with actions. Inter Milan were the opposition at that final hurdle and though their defensive capabilities were renowned, Celtic ran them ragged. After Gemmell's thunderbolt goal, the Italians had to chase the game and Chalmers made the game safe with five minutes still on the clock.

Celtic's European win in Lisbon had come in the same year that Third Lanark, the team that beat them in their very first Scottish Cup Final, went out of business – a victim, arguably, of the Old Firm's continued dominance and ability to suck up support from beyond Glasgow's boundaries. And it was also as a result of this that the face of Scottish football was changed irrevocably in 1975 with the restructuring of the League. Inevitably, neither Rangers nor Celtic has yet left the Premier Division.

A 4-0 Scottish Cup Final win against the old enemy in

1969 was the last hurrah of a great Celtic side which was perhaps nearing its sell-by date. As with post-Busby Manchester United, its rebuilding would tax a number of managers who followed, including former playing heroes Billy McNeill and David Hay.

LOSING GRIP

The 1970s were most memorable for the conclusion, in 1974, of that history-making sequence of nine League Championships in a row that had begun in 1966. Yet there was a steady and significant exodus of stars who, while playing international matches, discovered that Scots who'd moved south were often reaping greater rewards than those who stayed loyal to their Scottish clubs. Lou Macari, David Hay and – most disappointingly – Kenny Dalglish were among those migrating. Dalglish, however, showed loyalty in staying an extra two years before moving to Anfield.

The 1974-75 season that saw them lose their grip on the title, brought consolation in the shape of both domestic Cups, but the fact that Rangers – who'd won their own European title in 1972, albeit the less prestigious Cup Winners' Cup – took top honours undoubtedly hurt.

More serious, however, was the pain and

Left: Brian McClair won League and Cup medals on both sides of the border during his career with Celtic and Manchester United.

15

suffering Jock Stein suffered after being involved in a car crash in the summer of 1975. He would be obliged to take a season out of the spotlight and away from the sport's pressures – during which time team matters were left in the capable hands of his deputy, Sean Fallon – and his return for 1976-77 was celebrated with the Double.

This was Kenny Dalglish's swansong, while Danny McGrain supplied the class at the back. Yet McGrain who, like Stein, had fought back from serious injury in the form of a fractured skull, suffered an ankle injury after just seven games that kept him out for the season, and the loss of their two most influential players saw Celtic slump to fifth. Jock Stein took the decision to give way to former playing favourite Billy McNeill, who'd returned in 1975 and moved up the management ladder via Clyde and then Aberdeen.

TOP HONOURS

McNeill was the man in charge for the early part of the 1980s – a decade when a century of history was turned on its head. Both of the Glasgow giants had been caught by the passage of time and, while McNeill rebuilt, a duo commentators termed 'the New Firm' – Aberdeen and Dundee United – emerged to challenge the big city's dominance. Both challengers took their turn at honours, Alex Ferguson's Dons taking the Championship pennant

out of Glasgow for the first time since 1965 in 1980.

Celtic hit back and, with the goals of Charlie Nicholas a major factor, lifted the title in 1981. McNeill's side had garnered a trophy a season, and the title was retained thanks, in no small measure, to the introduction of young midfielder Paul McStay. However, European impact remained impossibly elusive and, as ever in the post-Stein era, this was the measure of the men who followed him in the Parkhead hot seat. McNeill believed the board were undervaluing him – several Premier League managers were said to be on better wages than he – and would quit to manage Manchester City.

He would be replaced by another ex-player, David Hay, who had to face life without the Arsenal-bound Charlie Nicholas. Happily, a replacement was already on the staff in the shape of the studious teenager Brain McClair, McNeill's final signing. He would prove excellent value for the £70,000 Celtic paid Motherwell for his services, finishing the club's top scorer in each of the four seasons he wore the hoops.

Hay's reign was an eventful one. Despite kicking off his first season in the League with five straight wins, the form couldn't be sustained and Aberdeen overhauled them. The campaign ended trophyless, only the third blank in 20 years, and Hay took action by signing Maurice Johnston from Watford for £400,000, a Scottish transfer record. He was ineligible for a Cup Winners' Cup game against Rapid Vienna that ended in controversy and had to be replayed at neutral Old Trafford, after a Rapid player claimed falsely to have been hit by a bottle.

Celtic lost the play-off, but came from behind in the Centenary Cup Final to deny Aberdeen the domestic Double. The 1985-86 season kicked off sadly with the death of Jock Stein, the legend, who passed away in September while managing the Scottish national team. It ended in drama too, but of a more palatable variety: a 16-game unbeaten run saw the Celts snatch the League from Hearts, who'd topped the table for a full five months but lacked the nerve to sustain their successful spell.

Billy McNeill was welcomed back in 1987 after four years in England with Manchester City and Aston Villa. Hay's final season had not been crowned with success of any kind despite an early League lead, surrendered to the newly resurgent Rangers. McNeill was to consistently come second best to his Rangers counterpart Graeme Souness, who set in motion a series of title wins that would, in 1997, equal Jock Stein's record.

Below: Yorkshire-born Mick McCarthy followed two years at Parkhead with managerial posts at Millwall and, currently, the Republic of Ireland.

16

Responding to this, the Celtic board went through managers as if discarding playing cards. Eire international Liam Brady had seen it all and done it all in a dramatically successful playing career, but Glasgow was hardly the place to learn the managerial ropes, despite the eventual arrival of Joe Jordan as his second-in-command. Brady reigned from the summer of 1991 to October 1993, spent around £6 million and ended up with nothing to show.

Even 1970s' hero Lou Macari – having earned his managerial spurs at Swindon, Birmingham, West Ham and

Stoke – failed to stimulate a Parkhead revival after arriving in October 1993. But he was the last appointment of the old board, and his days were numbered almost from the outset.

The hand now controlling the club's fortunes was millionaire Fergus McCann, who took control in 1994 after the club had suffered a close brush with financial catastrophe. Only with the return of ex-player Tommy Burns in July of that year as manager would fortunes pick up and a true challenge to Ibrox be mounted.

Above: Despite a creditable record of a goal every two games in a Celtic shirt, Maurice Johnston is best remembered as the first Catholic in modern times to sign for Rangers.

17

The Club Today

The return of Tommy Burns, who'd proved himself as a manager with Kilmarnock, was both optimistic and controversial. Optimistic because fans associated his never-say-die playing style with better days, and controversial because Celtic would eventually be fined a cool £100,000 for 'inducing'

Burns and assistant manager Billy Stark to break their contracts with Killie and make the move.

The feeling was, though, that 'Twist and Turns' would have crawled back to Parkhead on broken glass – which was reason enough to cheer. While Lou Macari had been a legend of rather longer ago, he'd never managed at the top level and some of his buys, like journeyman forward Wayne Biggins, 32, whom he knew from former club Stoke, had seemed to lack the qualities demanded by the denizens of Paradise.

Burns' rebuilding of the playing side was accompanied by a restructuring not only of the way the club was run but also of the ground where they played. The downside to this progress was the fact that, for the 1994-95 season, Celtic would cede home advantage by lodging at Hampden Park. Not that this at first seemed any kind of problem, as an 11-match unbeaten run was strung together and the League Cup Final reached. Then, as with Davie Hay's notorious season, things took a slump and the club suffered an equally long run without a win. Sadly, this was

Right: One of the smallest players to represent Celtic, winger Brian McLaughlin found it hard to press his claims for a regular first-team place among the high-priced imports.

Opposite: Stuart Gray shares his cultured left foot with father Eddie, a stalwart for Leeds United and Scotland.

to include the League Cup Final against Raith Rovers, managed by ex-Rangers man Jimmy Nicholl. And though Celtic dominated the match in possession terms, penalties were the way that it was decided.

Burns responded by throwing in the kids, using Bill Shankly's maxim that 'if they're good enough they're old enough'. New names like Donnelly, Mackay, Gray and McLaughlin were seen on the team sheet as the boss took stock of the talent available to him. His answer, later in the season, was to bolster his young squad with a number of shrewd foreign signings. The first of these was Pierre Van Hooijdonk, the towering centre-forward signed from Holland's team of the season, NAC Breda.

CUP TRIUMPH

It would be the Flying Dutchman who would propel Celtic towards their first trophy in six years, the Scottish Cup, in which they triumphed over Airdrie. At the back, Albanian Rudi Vata was added to a defence already boasting Tommy Boyd and Mark McNally, while as a last line of defence the legendary Packy Bonner's place was being threatened by a newcomer in ex-Falkirk keeper Gordon Marshall.

Burns wasn't about to splash out willy-nilly, as a bank overdraft reported at £5 million was unlikely to go away in a hurry. Nevertheless, Van Hooijdonk proved well worth the £1.3 million investment, his decisive Final goal ensuring Celtic would enjoy European competition in 1995-96's Cup Winners' Cup. But he realised that the Championship remained the main aim, especially with Rangers regarding it as their own private property.

With this in mind, the manager entered the transfer market once again as Celtic prepared to return to Parkhead. The club's record signing, £2.2 million German Andy Thom, was quickly into action, scoring in just his second League game. Bought to partner Van Hooijdonk up front, he'd prove as much a provider as a goaltaker. His second League strike came in a 3-3 draw with old rivals Rangers in November, proving he had the big-match temperament that Glasgow derbies demand.

Thom's influence as a playmaker would be sorely needed, with the decision of John Collins to seek pastures new and play the coming season in Monaco. His six years with Celtic had seen the ex-Hibernian man mature into an international-class prospect who matched a will to win with no little skill. He would clearly be missed. Paul McStay, however, was still very much part of the fabric of the side and an inspirational captain now coming up to his 14th year with a club he and his forebears had served with such distinction.

The European Cup Winners' Cup campaign was

to prove a short one. Despite demolishing Dynamo Batumi on a 7-2 aggregate, Andreas Thom providing the lion's share of those goals with a brace home and away, they found their path barred by Paris St Germain. The French aces scored the only goal in Glasgow, adding three more at the Parc Des Princes to emphasise the gap in class that still existed between Celtic and the cream of Europe.

WORLD CLASS

Back home, the record book showed that the season belonged not to Burns' Bhoys but to Rangers, who completed their third League and Cup Double of the 1990s. Yet Celtic's amazing undefeated League run which began back in October and extended to the end of the season, gave their fans cause to cheer and their neighbours something to think about. The form of Van Hooijdonk was clearly the catalyst, but it was when Jorge Cadete threw in his lot with the hoops, having quit Sporting Lisbon in despair, that things began to ignite. He hit his first goal for the Bhoys against Aberdeen in an emphatic 5-0 victory, underlining Celtic's intention of improving on the second place they'd held since October.

Suddenly, Parkhead was becoming just as cosmopolitan as Ibrox – and even more was to come. Glasgow football had become the envy of the world and when Italian ace Paulo De Canio came to the city in 1996, the first phone call he received was from former AC

Opposite: German international Andreas Thom was one of the 1990s' earlier foreign arrivals at Parkhead.

Above left: Widely tipped to be returning to his native Merseyside, ex-Bolton defender Alan Stubbs made Glasgow his destination in 1996.

21

notching in five of those games to prove he was carrying on where he'd left off the previous season.

Yet the pattern of the coming campaign was set by the game at Ibrox on 28 September that brought the first League defeat. As before, it was Celtic's inability to register a League win over the boys in blue that cost them the title. Before, it had been one loss and three draws – this time round all four slipped away. True, the home games were by a single goal but it was to the wrong team.

Only three other teams bested the Bhoys in League combat, however, and there never seemed any danger they'd be overtaken for the runner's-up spot. Di Canio, who'd rightly be acclaimed as the Scottish Player of the Year, was magnificent, bringing a flair to the forward play that had been sorely needed. Unfortunately, his ability to supply big Pierre was cruelly cut short when the striker was transferred to Nottingham Forest.

Wage demands, the perennial Celtic complaint that had seen stars go south since the 1970s, were supposedly the reason for Van Hooijdonk's departure but the fans were far from happy. He'd won their hearts and minds in the short time he'd starred for Celtic, inspiring many chants. Ironically, he could not save his new side from relegation, while young hopeful Simon Donnelly was among those hoping to take his place in the hoops.

SUCCESS STORY

Donnelly was one of several players to make a mark during the season – but the big success story in terms of home-grown talent was Stuart Kerr, a goalkeeper whose fine form kept Gordon Marshall out almost all season until, in April, he dislocated a finger and let the more experienced man finish the campaign between the sticks. Kerr was undoubtedly one for the future.

After those four distressing League losses, the big payback came in the Scottish Cup Semi-Final when a Malky Mackay strike and a Di Canio penalty saw the Celts triumphant over their Old Firm rivals – a win that surely opened the way to silverware. Their opponents in the showcase game were Falkirk, and it scarcely seemed possible that they could fail to overturn a side that would end the season marooned in the middle of the First Division. Yet, as so often happens in Cup competitions, the form-book was completely rewritten as David toppled Goliath with a single goal.

This one result was enough to set the rumour mill grinding, and it was suggested that the Burns era might well be at an end. Not everybody believed this could be so: after all, second in anyone else's language is far from failure. Yet it was true. Rather than accept what was tantamount to demotion, Burns walked out of his beloved Parkhead just before the end of the season, leaving stricken players and supporters behind him.

There was little doubt that Burns' Celtic had trailed in second to a better team – but one, conversely, with more resources at their disposal than he had. In Cadete and Di Canio, he'd introduced two outstanding international-class

Above: Stuart Kerr graduated from the reserves to displace Gordon Marshall as Celtic's Number 1 in the 1996-97 season.

Opposite: Along with Jorge Cadete, Italian Paolo Di Canio added flair and bite to the Bhoys' attack, but his volatile relationship with club management gave cause for concern.

Milan team-mate Roberto Baggio who asked him to get him a Celtic shirt. Far from being a local squabble, the Old Firm was clearly a worldwide phenomenon.

Burns' third season in charge was the one everyone thought would see the corner turned. And it was imperative that it was. Should Rangers take the title, they would have equalled Jock Stein's nine in a row, so the motivation of the players and the enthusiasm of the fans was at an even higher pitch than usual when hostilities commenced. All started well with five wins out of six games, Hibernian and Dunfermline suffering five-goal thrashings. Van Hooijdonk, too, was in fantastic form,

players to Scottish football, and there were many new younger faces in the squad that made pundits belive that Celtic were better placed than ever to stop the rot and prevent their 24-year-old record being eclipsed.

But Fergus McCann, the man who mattered, clearly did not agree. Kenny Dalglish, that wily old ex-Celt now manager of Newcastle, was quick to put his cards on the table by moving to add Tommy to the coaching staff at St James' Park, believing the man had something to offer the side that had finished second south of the border. A summer of confusion was on the cards as candidates for the Parkhead job jostled for position in the press.

Something sadly all too certain on the playing side was the retirement of Paul McStay, who made the decision to hang up his boots after an injury-ravaged season, but Cadete and Di Canio's future with the club seemed in

doubt. The identity of the new manager was also shrouded in confusion, most of the money having been placed on Wimbledon manager Joe Kinnear – tellingly, a man who'd created much from slim resources at Wimbledon. As an ex-Eire international, he would clearly fit the Celtic mould and, unlike another of that ilk, Liam Brady, he'd bring a track record with him.

But the man who eventually succeeded to the top job in late June was Brown – not Craig, the current Scottish manager, but his brother Jock, 51. He'd combined a career as a television commentator with a business dispensing legal advice to top Scottish managers, but had somehow avoided taking on a managerial post himself. It was an unusual appointment, to say the least, but no one at Celtic could afford to be surprised after the events of recent years. One could only hope that Jock Stein, looking down,

would give the new boss his blessing and that Brown would be the man to lead the Celts once again to glory.

Sensibly, Brown would be looking after the contracts and public relations side of things rather than attempting to switch roles from commentator to coach. The job of rejuvenating the club's fortunes on the pitch fell to Wim Jansen, a Dutchman best known for a playing career with Feyenoord whose last coaching job had been in the Japanese J-League.

He lost no time in surrounding himself with local knowledge in the shape of former players from several generations: Lisbon Lion John Clark, 1970s giant and one-time manager David Hay and, last but not least, ten-year absentee Murdo MacLeod. He had gained managerial experience with Partick Thistle since leaving Celtic and would be Jansen's assistant.

The mettle of the new management team was soon to

be put to the test on two fronts, as they simultaneously steered their team to a UEFA Cup First Leg win over Inter Cable-Tel of Wales and attempted to cope with want-away pair Cadete and Di Canio. The 3-0 win in Cardiff saw £1 million man Darren Jackson from Hibs make his debut as substitute, while Andy Thom and Dane Morten Weighorst, standing in for the two absentees, both scored to emphasise their intention of playing a part in Celtic's future plans.

It seemed inevitable that many future names on the team sheet would also be European – Dutch for preference, as Jansen returned to the market he knew in search of bargains. This was a tactic that had yet to fail the other side of Glasgow, and after so many years of struggle there seemed little doubt that Celtic's faithful fans would cheer eleven Martians to the echo were they to bring the League pennant back to Celtic Park once more.

Player Profiles

GOALKEEPERS
Packy Bonner, Gordon Marshall, Ronnie Simpson.

DEFENDERS
Tommy Boyd, Jim Brogan, Tommy Burns, John Clark, Jim Craig, Tommy Gemmell, David Hay, Danny McGrain, Billy McNeill, Tony Mowbray, Jock Stein.

MIDFIELDERS
Roy Aitken, Bertie Auld, Bobby Collins, John Collins, Bobby Evans, Peter Grant, Murdo MacLeod, Paul McStay, Bobby Murdoch, Davie Provan.

STRIKERS
Steve Chalmers, George Connelly, Paolo Di Canio, Kenny Dalglish, Harry Hood, John 'Yogi' Hughes, Mo Johnston, Jimmy Johnstone, Bobby Lennox, Lou Macari, Frank McAvennie, Brian McClair, George McCluskey, Frank McGarvey, Jimmy McGrory, John McPhail, Charlie Nicholas, Pierre Van Hooijdonk.

There have been some doughty performers lined up in the green and white hoops over the years. This book hopefully brings you closer, in words and pictures, to some of the most celebrated Celts ever to have represented the club. But have you thought about what you could do if you could select from all those featured?

Imagine Jimmy Johnstone feeding crosses from the wing for a twin strike force of Nicholas and McGrory to convert…or a back four of McGrain, McNeill, Stein and Gemmell? The legendary Bobby Evans could link in midfield with Paul McStay, or we could return John Collins from the Principality with the reward of plying his trade alongside that idiosyncratic performer Bertie Auld.

All in all, the possibilities are endless, except in the goalkeeping department where just three custodians vie for the shirt. But even then, how do you choose between Ronnie Simpson, the Lisbon Lion, and the long-serving Packy Bonner? We'll leave it up to you!

25

Roy Aitken

PERSONAL FILE

Born: 24 November 1958
Birthplace: Irvine
Height: 6' 0"
Weight: 13st 0lb

LEAGUE RECORD

FROM-TO	CLUB	APPS	GOALS
1975-90	Celtic	483	40
1990-91	Newcastle Utd	54	1
1991-92	St Mirren	34	1
1992-95	Aberdeen	29	2
Total		600	44

CELTIC LEAGUE DEBUT

21 February 1976 v Aberdeen

SCOTLAND DEBUT

12 September 1979 v Peru

SCOTLAND HONOURS

1979-80	5
1980-81	—
1981-82	—
1982-83	3
1983-84	3
1984-85	2
1985-86	10
1986-87	7
1987-88	9
1988-89	8
1989-90	9
1990-91	—
1991-92	1
Total	57

DID YOU KNOW?

On returning to Parkhead for Packy Bonner's testimonial in May 1991, Roy's arrival on the pitch was greeted by a huge roar of approval from the crowd.

'That boy will play for Scotland one day', was Jock Stein's quote after watching Roy Aitken play for the first time as a skinny 13-year-old. The lad went on to prove the Big Man right more than 50 times – many of them as captain – during a glittering career which saw him turn out for Celtic over three different decades. Robert 'Roy' Aitken made his debut for Celtic in 1976, four years after his move to Parkhead from Ayr United's Boys' Club.

An inspirational leader, Aitken was looked on as the ideal replacement for recently-retired Billy McNeill and, once he got his name on that team-sheet, there was no way he was going to be easily dislodged. He was to become a regular fixture in the side for the next 14 years, averaging over 40 games a term, and quickly became a firm favourite of the Parkhead fans. His uncompromising manner and sheer physical strength and presence earned him the nickname of 'The Bear'.

Equally effective at full-back, central defence or sweeper, it was in the holding role in front of Roddie MacDonald, and later Tom McAdam, that Roy was to prove most valuable. Despite his robust approach – though Scotland coach Andy Roxburgh once described him as 'gazelle-like' – Aitken was a brilliant reader of the game, who could spot an opening long before it existed and, with one telling pass, immediately turn defence into attack.

Like a number of his predecessors, a place on the Celtic coaching staff looked assured for Aitken. However, after 667 appearances for the club (during which time he scored 55 goals and amassed five League Championship medals, four Scottish Cups and one League Cup badge) he moved to Newcastle United at the beginning of 1990. He returned north to pursue a career in management, first with St Mirren and then Aberdeen, where he took over as manager in 1994.

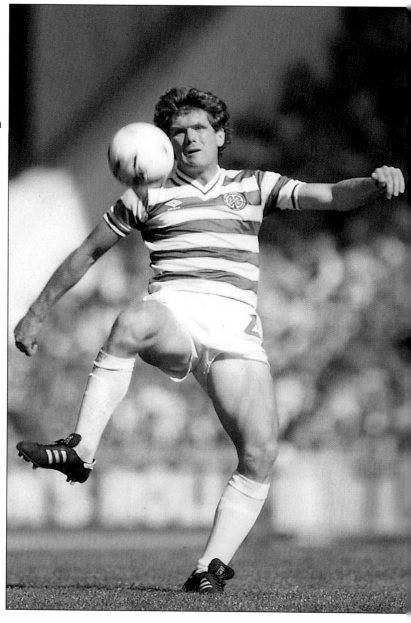

1955-1961 & 1965-1971

Bertie Auld

PERSONAL FILE

Born: 23 March 1938
Birthplace: Maryhill
Height: 5' 8"
Weight: 10st 10lb

LEAGUE RECORD

FROM-TO	CLUB	APPS	GOALS
1955-61	Celtic	50	15
1961-65	Birmingham C	125	26
1965-71	Celtic	126	38
1971-73	Hibernian	n/k	n/k
Total		301	79

CELTIC LEAGUE DEBUT

7 September 1957 v Falkirk

SCOTLAND DEBUT

7 May 1958 v Hungary

SCOTLAND HONOURS

Season	Caps
1957-58	1
1958-59	1
1959-60	1
Total	3

STAR QUOTE

'He could take two or three people out of the game with a pass.'
SEAN FALLON

Jock Stein can rightly lay claim to turning a moderately talented bunch of individuals into the most skilful and feared side in Europe, but it was his predecessor who laid the foundation for Celtic's meteoric rise, with the acquisition of Bertie Auld three months before Stein's arrival in January 1965. Quite simply, he was the greatest-ever Celtic signing, after Jimmy McGrory's right-hand man Sean Fallon persuaded the Parkhead board to take a chance on 'Ten Thirty', a player who had been off-loaded to Birmingham City four seasons earlier.

He possessed the sweetest left foot ever seen at Parkhead and, along with Bobby Murdoch, formed the backbone of the side which was to dominate the game north of the border for the best part of ten years. Auld was a genius with the ball, his value in today's over-inflated transfer market cannot be contemplated, little 20-yard bursts interspersed with Exocet-like crossfield balls, more often than not to Jimmy Johnstone.

Auld, who helped win five Championships, three Scottish Cups, four League Cups and the European Cup in 1967 was – surprisingly – allowed to leave in 1971 for Hibernian, a club he later managed without great success. Spells in charge at Partick Thistle (twice), Hamilton Accies and Dumbarton followed, before he called time on his football career late in 1988 to concentrate on running his Glasgow pub.

A keen practical joker, Auld could always be relied on to keep the spirits up in the dressing room. When, on the 30th anniversary of Celtic's greatest night in Europe, he was asked to compare the Lisbon Lions with the current Rangers side sweeping all before them in Scotland, he thought for a few moments before answering, 'I think we'd win, probably 2-1. It would be close, but you must remember most of us are well over 50 now!'

1978-1995

Pat 'Packy' Bonner

Jock Stein's eye for spotting real talent was legendary, but when it came to goalkeepers his judgement was sometimes questionable – although it was never said to his face. He even off-loaded Ronnie Simpson to Celtic shortly before making the trip to Paradise himself in 1965, but there is no doubt he got it spot on when making 'Packy' Bonner his final signing in May 1978.

Bonner, who was also a highly useful Gaelic footballer, was spotted playing soccer for Leicester City's youth team and very little persuasion was required to entice him over from his home in Co Donegal, Ireland. He made the Number 1 jersey his own at the start of the 1980-81 season, after Peter Latchford suffered a training accident.

Not always blessed with the cream of the defensive world in front of him, Packy – a master shot-stopper with few peers in a one-on-one situation – went on to collect four League Championship, one League Cup and two Scottish Cup medals in a career which saw him turn out over 600 times for the club.

However, it will probably be for his heroics at international level that Bonner will best be remembered. A member of the great Jack Charlton side of the late 1980s and early 1990s, Packy broke the hearts of England fans with his best-ever game between the sticks for club or country in the 1988 European

Championships in Stuttgart. A string of stunning stops, two in particular from Gary Lineker, earned the Republic a quarter-final passage, while a penalty shoot-out save against Romania guaranteed the Irish another last-eight spot at the World Cup finals of Italia '90.

Packy, who went on to win a then record 80 caps for his country, was freed by manager Lou Macari in May 1994 but was persuaded to stay, although little pressure was needed, when new boss Tommy Burns took over the reins months later.

Tommy Boyd

PERSONAL FILE

Born: 24 November 1965
Birthplace: Glasgow
Height: 5' 11"
Weight: 11st 4lb

LEAGUE RECORD

FROM-TO	CLUB	APPS	GOALS
1983-91	Motherwell	252	6
1991-92	Chelsea	23	—
1992-97	Celtic	193	2
Total		468	8

CELTIC LEAGUE DEBUT

8 February 1992 v Aidrie

SCOTLAND DEBUT

12 September 1990 v Romania

SCOTLAND HONOURS

SEASON	CAPS
1990-91	4
1991-92	6
1992-93	7
1993-94	4
1994-95	6
1995-96	11
1996-97	8
Total	46

DID YOU KNOW?
Tommy was the captain who lifted the Cup when Motherwell beat Dundee United 4-3 at Hampden in 1991.

Very little of Liam Brady's time in charge of Celtic will be remembered with affection, although the acquisition of Tommy Boyd certainly bucked the trend of his two-year tenure. Born in Glasgow in November 1965, the cultured left-back already had a Scottish Cup winner's medal and over 250 appearances for Motherwell behind him when he left to join Chelsea, following his side's 1991 success over Dundee United.

But he failed to settle with the Londoners and his unhappy eight-month stay, which saw him play just 23 times, was ended when Brady agreed a swop deal with counterpart Ian Porterfield for Parkhead misfit Tony Cascarino. Boyd, once a rock at the heart of Motherwell's rearguard, was revealed as a masterful playmaker, comfortable with either foot and an instant hit with the fans of the club he supported as a boy.

Further success followed for Boyd, who was converted to the right side of defence by new boss Tommy Burns, when he picked up his second Scottish Cup winner's medal following the 1-0 defeat of Airdrie at Hampden in May 1995. As Jackie McNamara and Tosh McKinlay arrived to fill the full-back berths, Boyd formed a positively Scrooge-like partnership with John Hughes at the centre of the defence.

Boyd, a Scotland regular with over 40 caps, was ever-present for his country during the Euro '96 campaign, culminating with the Finals in England where he performed heroically at the back, alongside Blackburn's Colin Hendry. With the arrival of Alan Stubbs, Boyd (who has few peers when it comes to the reading of a game) moved back to a sweeper-cum-libero role, a position he looks destined to fill for a several years to come.

Jim Brogan

PERSONAL FILE

Born: 5 June 1944
Birthplace: Glasgow
Height: 5' 10"
Weight: 11st 3lb

LEAGUE RECORD

FROM-TO	CLUB	APPS	GOALS
1962-75	Celtic	212	6
1975-77	Coventry C	28	—
1977	Ayr Utd	n/k	n/k
Total		240	6

CELTIC LEAGUE DEBUT

21 September 1963 v Falkirk

SCOTLAND DEBUT

21 April 1971 v Portugal

SCOTLAND HONOURS

SEASON	CAPS
1970-71	4
Total	4

DID YOU KNOW?
As well as being an accomplished footballer, Jim was an accountant by profession.

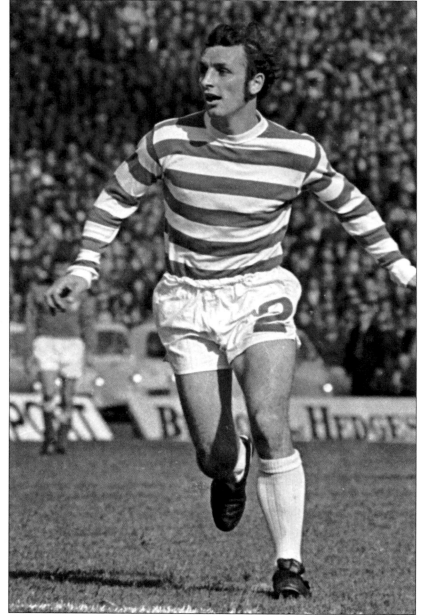

A stylish defender who was always overshadowed by the bigger names in the team at the time, Jim Brogan was unfortunate in that he came into the Celtic team at the same time as Kenny Dalglish, Lou Macari, George Connelly and Danny McGrain were all making their names.

He'd served quite a long 'apprenticeship' before becoming a first-team regular, succeeding John Clark in the Number 6 shirt and was, in fact, rather older than the aforementioned wave of players who replaced the Lisbon Lions.

However, he was still considered a first-team regular by Jock Stein in the late 1960s and early 1970s and picked up several domestic honours before being given a free transfer in 1975.

Brogan fitted the Celtic mould at left-half and enjoyed cantering up the park to join the attack whenever he could. He even chipped in with a couple of goals, although he could never have been described as a goalscorer by instinct. As George Connelly laid claim to his position, he slipped back to Number 3 to enjoy two more successful seasons and pick up a fourth Scottish Cup medal.

A Celtic fan as a boy, Brogan was recognised by the Parkhead faithful as one of them and was always a favourite with supporters. He was good enough to play for the Scottish League against their English counterparts in 1969 and won full international honours the following year. Sadly his fourth and last game in a Scotland shirt saw him sustain a broken leg, and he was unable to reclaim his international place.

Captaining the Celtic team in his final match against arch-enemies Rangers in May 1975, he enjoyed a season and a half with Coventry before returning north for a brief swansong with Ayr. He's since become a successful businessman with a million-pound empire.

Tommy Burns

PERSONAL FILE

Born: 16 December 1956
Birthplace: Glasgow
Height: 5' 11"
Weight: 11st 3lb

LEAGUE RECORD

FROM-TO	CLUB	APPS	GOALS
1975-89	Celtic	357	52
1989-94	Kilmarnock	151	16
Total		508	68

CELTIC LEAGUE DEBUT

19 April 1975 v Dundee

SCOTLAND DEBUT

19 May 1981 v Northern Ireland

SCOTLAND HONOURS

SEASON	CAPS
1980-81	1
1981-82	2
1982-83	4
1983-84	—
1984-85	—
1985-86	—
1986-87	—
1987-88	1
Total	8

STAR QUOTE
'Burns does the simple things effectively.'
JOCK STEIN

Tommy Burns only ever had one ambition in life and that was to play for Glasgow Celtic. Growing up in the tough Calton district of the East End of Glasgow, the fiery redhead could never have imagined that he would one day manage the side he had dreamed of playing for. 'Twist and Turns', as he was affectionately known, was first and foremost a Celtic fan, as well as a devout Catholic and devoted family man.

A superbly gifted midfielder, with the sweetest left foot seen at Parkhead since the days of Bertie Auld, Burns had the ability to prise open any defence with a precision pass or mazy dribble which, in full flight, was reminiscent of Jimmy Johnstone in his heyday. The fact that he only accrued eight international caps remains a mystery, amplified by the fact that Jock Stein, who brought the skinny little teenager to Parkhead, was in charge of the Scotland side when Tommy was at the peak of his career.

During his time at Celtic, Burns played in exactly 500 games in all competitions – he was rewarded with six Championship medals and three Scottish Cup medals before he departed for Kilmarnock in December 1989. The Parkhead fans loved Burns, and 45,000 of them turned up for his testimonial against Liverpool in August 1987. It was only a matter of time before he returned as boss and, after guiding Kilmarnock into the Premier Division in 1993, he was summoned 'home' to pick up the pieces following the disastrous reigns of Liam Brady and Lou Macari.

In the fans' eyes, Burns was the only candidate for the job. But the surrender of the club's cherished nine-in-a-row record to their greatest rivals Rangers in 1997 brought a premature end to his stay in Paradise. Supporters wept openly as he walked out of Parkhead for the final time, many feeling a grave sense of injustice that he had not been given enough time to finish the job.

1959-1971

Steve Chalmers

PERSONAL FILE

Born: 26 December 1936
Birthplace: Glasgow
Height: 5' 9"
Weight: 10st 12lb

LEAGUE RECORD

FROM-TO	CLUB	APPS	GOALS
1959-71	Celtic	261	155
1971-72	Morton	n/k	n/k
1972-75	Partick Thistle	n/k	n/k
Total		261	155

CELTIC LEAGUE DEBUT

10 March 1959 v Airdrie

SCOTLAND DEBUT

3 October 1964 v Wales

SCOTLAND HONOURS

SEASON	CAPS
1964-65	2
1965-66	2
1966-67	1
Total	5

DID YOU KNOW?

Steve played for Newmarket Town while completing his National Service.

Steve Chalmers enjoyed many highs while wearing the famous hoops, but it will be for one golden moment in Lisbon in 1967 that he is most fondly remembered by Celtic fans. A lethal two-footed striker who was blessed with the speed of an Olympic athlete – he was timed at under 11 seconds for a 100-yard dash – Chalmers earned his rightful place in the record-books with the 85th-minute goal that finally ended the dogged resistance of Inter Milan in the famous European Cup Final victory of that year.

Born in Glasgow on Boxing Day 1936, Chalmers joined Celtic after representing his country at junior level, from top non-League club Ashfield in February 1959. Stevie, often used as an orthodox winger on either side of the park, had the pace and eye for goal to prise open the best defences, but it was not until he was switched to his favoured centre-forward role by Jock Stein that the best of the likeable hitman was seen.

Chalmers won five full caps for Scotland, including a memorable 1-1 draw against Brazil in 1966 which saw him get his name on the international scoresheet for the first time with a first-minute goal. In addition, he collected five League Championship, three Scottish Cup and five League Cup medals, plus his European Cup badge of 1967, during his 12-year stay at Parkhead.

A wonderful solo goal in the 4-0 Scottish Cup Final drubbing of Rangers in 1969 cemented Stevie's position as an idol of the Parkhead faithful – but, just five months later, his career suffered an almost fatal knock when he broke his leg in the 1969 League Cup Final victory over St Johnstone.

Stevie departed from Parkhead after 405 appearances and 228 goals for the club to become player-coach at Morton. This was followed by a short spell at Partick Thistle, after which he returned to Parkhead to head the successful Celtic Development Pools agency.

John Clark

PERSONAL FILE

Born: 13 March 1941
Birthplace: Bellshill
Height: 5' 8"
Weight: 11st 5lb

LEAGUE RECORD

FROM-TO	CLUB	APPS	GOALS
1958	Birmingham C	—	—
1958-71	Celtic	185	—
1971-73	Morton	n/k	n/k
Total		185	—

CELTIC LEAGUE DEBUT

3 October 1959 v Arbroath

SCOTLAND DEBUT

25 June 1966 v Brazil

SCOTLAND HONOURS

SEASON	CAPS
1965-66	1
1966-67	3
Total	4

DID YOU KNOW?
He was the second John Clark to wear a Celtic shirt after a Clyde striker who played two games on loan in 1903.

Regarded by most Celtic fans as a quiet achiever, John Clark was a central defender of real quality but one who shunned the limelight in favour of being a vital cog in Celtic's greatest-ever side. Nowadays, when people speak of the 1967 Lisbon Lions, names such as Jimmy Johnstone, Billy McNeill and Tommy Gemmell trip off many a tongue. However, Clark was coolly efficient and equally as important. Older fans believe the legendary Billy McNeill would never have been half the player he was had Clark not been around to cover his back.

The fact may have been lost to many, but Jock Stein was a man with an eye for talent. Clark joined Celtic from Larkhall Thistle in 1958 and began his career in the hoops as a traditional left-half. However, Stein recognised the player's strengths and understanding of the game and immediately installed him as a sweeper.

A player with immaculate positional sense, Clark was also immensely cool under pressure. His telepathic understanding with McNeill was the cornerstone on which Celtic's European triumph of '67 was built. However, he was the first of the Lisbon Lions to be supplanted by a younger man – in this case, Jim Brogan.

Clark left to join Morton in the early 1970s but retired from playing soon after. He re-entered the game as assistant manager at Aberdeen and later Celtic between 1978 and 1983 as McNeill's right-hand man – as he had been on the pitch for many years. He's since guided the fortunes of Cowdenbeath, Stranraer and Clyde in the lower divisions, but will never be forgotten at Parkhead.

Bobby Collins

PERSONAL FILE

Born: 16 February 1931
Birthplace: Govanhill
Height: 5' 4"
Weight: 9st 6lb

LEAGUE RECORD

FROM-TO	CLUB	APPS	GOALS
1949-58	Celtic	220	80
1958-62	Everton	133	42
1962-67	Leeds Utd	149	24
1967-69	Bury	75	5
1969-71	Morton	n/k	n/k
1972	Oldham Ath	7	—
Total		584	151

CELTIC LEAGUE DEBUT

10 September 1949 v Queen of the South

SCOTLAND DEBUT

21 October 1950 v Wales

SCOTLAND HONOURS

SEASON	CAPS
1950-51	3
1951-52	—
1952-53	—
1953-54	—
1954-55	3
1955-56	2
1956-57	6
1957-58	8
1958-59	6
1959-60	—
1960-61	—
1961-62	—
1962-63	—
1963-64	—
1964-65	3
Total	31

DID YOU KNOW?

Between his spells at Morton and Oldham, Bobby was player-coach with Australian sides Ringwood City, Hakoah and Wilhelmina.

Midfield general Bobby Collins belied his diminutive stature with a towering talent. His departure from Parkhead in 1958 (the proceeds of his sale, it's rumoured, going to pay for new floodlights) was much mourned, but it was in the twilight of his career that he made his greatest mark as captain and hub of Don Revie's great Leeds side of the 1960s.

Originally a winger when he arrived at Parkhead, it was when he moved inside that Collins exerted his greatest influence on the game. He was also an ice-cool penalty taker, scoring an unique hat-trick of them in 1953 against Aberdeen; his skill with the dead ball was further illustrated by his legendary 'one-step' corner kicks, delivered accurately with scarcely a run-up.

Having helped Celtic to many honours in the 1950s, kicking off with the Scottish Cup win of 1951, he was a key ingredient of the Double-winning team of 1954 despite missing the Cup Final itself. He also won League Cup medals in 1957 and 1958.

Everton didn't see the best of him but, after captaining Leeds to the Second Division title, Collins was voted English Footballer of the Year in 1965 as United narrowly failed to take the Double. He was also recalled to the Scottish side after a six-year absence.

A broken thigh, sustained in a European Cup game in October 1965, was hard to overcome at nearly 35 and he played out his days in lower levels before managing Hull and Barnsley.

John Collins

PERSONAL FILE

Born: 31 January 1968
Birthplace: Galashiels
Height: 5' 7"
Weight: 10st 10lb

LEAGUE RECORD

FROM-TO	CLUB	APPS	GOALS
1984-90	Hibernian	163	16
1990-96	Celtic	217	47
1996-97	Monaco	n/k	n/k
Total		380	63

CELTIC LEAGUE DEBUT

25 August 1990 v Motherwell

SCOTLAND DEBUT

17 February 1988 v Saudi Arabia

SCOTLAND HONOURS

1987-88	1
1988-89	—
1989-90	3
1990-91	2
1991-92	2
1992-93	6
1993-94	4
1994-95	7
1995-96	11
1996-97	6
Total	42

DID YOU KNOW?

John scored on his international debut in the 2-2 draw with Saudi Arabia.

Celtic were forced to pay Hibernian £920,000 to bring gifted midfielder John Collins back to Parkhead in July 1990, after letting him slip through the net as a raw 16-year-old. Born in Galashiels in 1968, Collins gained rave reviews for his performances with Celtic Boys' Club before he was, surprisingly, allowed to leave for non-League Hutcheson Vale. From there, he was promptly snapped up by Hibs in 1984.

Collins established himself in the Edinburgh club's first team the following season, and his superb vision and close control soon had scouts from the country's leading clubs filling the Easter Road stands week in, week out. Scotland recognition followed for a player whose ball-winning skills and lethal long-range shooting tempted Billy McNeill to part with nearly £1 million when the player arrived home from the World Cup Finals in 1990.

Collins soon formed a telepathic understanding with international team-mate Paul McStay, but a lack of class forwards frequently saw the pair's best efforts count for nothing. Restricted to just one domestic honour – the Scottish Cup in 1995 – Collins decided to head for pastures new.

The arrival of top Europeans Pierre Van Hooijdonk, Jorge Cadete and Andreas Thom failed to persuade him that the good times were just around the corner at Parkhead and, as a free agent, he headed for Monaco in the summer of 1996.

Collins, an arch-critic of the bruising nature of Scottish football, revelled in the time and space afforded to him in the French First Division and a Championship medal was captured in his first season in the Principality.

His departure from Parkhead was far from harmonious, although the fans' anger was directed more at the club for failing to offer Collins, by then closing in on his 40th cap, a deal that could have tempted him to stay.

George Connelly

PERSONAL FILE

Born: 1 March 1949
Birthplace: Fife
Height: 6' 1"
Weight: 12st 0lb

LEAGUE RECORD

FROM-TO	CLUB	APPS	GOALS
1964-75	Celtic	136	5
1975-76	Falkirk (loan)	n/k	n/k
Total		136	5

CELTIC LEAGUE DEBUT

30 April 1968 v Dunfermline Athletic

SCOTLAND DEBUT

17 October 1973 v Czechoslovakia

SCOTLAND HONOURS

SEASON	CAPS
1973-74	2
Total	2

DID YOU KNOW?

Described by some as Celtic's Beckenbauer, George returned to Tulliallan Thistle for a second spell in August 1978.

The sight of George Connelly stroking the ball into an empty Hampden net in April 1969 will be forever etched in the minds of all Celtic fans. But, sadly for the Parkhead faithful, it was a spectacle they were to witness all too infrequently as one of the greatest talents of the day was lost to the game, long before he fulfilled his undoubted potential.

George Connelly had it all. A central defender with an eye for goal, he was seen as the ideal replacement for skipper Billy McNeill and a glittering future surely lay ahead. Celtic fans were given their first glimpse of his talents when, as a 15-year-old, he displayed nerves of steel to keep the ball in the air the entire way round the Parkhead pitch before a vital European Cup Winners' Cup clash against Dynamo Kiev in January 1966.

Connelly broke into the first team in 1968 and when he robbed John Greig on the edge of the Rangers box to slot home the third goal in the 4-0 Scottish Cup Final drubbing of Rangers the following April, he ensured his place in the hearts of the Bhoys' fans.

Connelly was maturing as a ball-winning playmaker with distribution to match that of master craftsman Bertie Auld, and his growing reputation was further enhanced when he grabbed the only goal of the 1970 European Cup semi-final first leg victory over Leeds United at Elland Road.

However, Connelly, who played 254 times for the club in all competitions and won the first of his two Scotland caps in a World Cup qualifier against Czechoslovakia, was far from happy in the spotlight. Claiming he could no longer take the pressures associated with the job, he walked out of the club in November 1973.

He was never the same player again and shortly after his return to the ranks broke his ankle in a European Cup clash against Basle of Switzerland in March 1974, and again his faith in the sport was tested.

Connelly helped Celtic pick up four Scottish League titles, three Scottish Cups and two League Cups, and was awarded Player of the Year in 1973, before his rare talent was lost to the club for good when he was freed from his contract in September 1975.

Jim Craig

PERSONAL FILE

Born: 30 April 1943
Birthplace: Glasgow
Height: 6' 0"
Weight: 11st 0lb

LEAGUE RECORD

FROM-TO	CLUB	APPS	GOALS
1965-72	Celtic	149	1
1972-74	Sheffield Wed	6	—
Total		155	1

CELTIC LEAGUE DEBUT

13 November 1965 v St Johnstone

SCOTLAND DEBUT

22 November 1967 v Wales

SCOTLAND HONOURS

SEASON	CAPS
1967-68	1
Total	1

DID YOU KNOW?
Between his periods with Celtic and the Owls, Jim enjoyed a spell with South African side Hellenic.

Lisbon Lion Craig is probably the only dentist ever to don the hoops. The full-back was almost as well-known for his dental studies as his football career, which won him more medals than most, including a European Cup badge. He combined his University studies with a footballer's life until summer 1966 and became a first-team regular soon after.

An incredible 14 domestic honours came his

way in a seven-year Parkhead career which ended after the 6-1 Scottish Cup Final win over Hibs in 1972. Craig was always better coming forward than defending, and it was he who played the ball to fellow full-back Tommy Gemmell to score the equaliser against Inter Milan in 1967.

He relished the big stage and once admitted he needed pressure to make him play better. Craig was a hard tackler who could also use the ball well but was surprisingly only capped once by Scotland, who weren't exactly blessed with an abundance of good right-backs at the time. He moved on to Sheffield Wednesday after his Parkhead days were over, but played only two part-seasons at Hillsborough before hanging up his boots.

A spell as Waterford's manager followed, but dentistry was always his preferred career choice. His sons currently play top-class rugby in Scotland, and he confesses he has more interest in watching them play than following football in the 1990s.

Only the great Danny McGrain could be classed as a better right-back than Jim Craig, who will rightly remembered as a Celtic great.

Paolo Di Canio

PERSONAL FILE

Born: 9 July 1968
Birthplace: Rome
Height: 5' 10"
Weight: 11st 0lb

LEAGUE RECORD

FROM-TO	CLUB	APPS	GOALS
1993-94	Napoli	26	5
1994-96	AC Milan	37	6
1996-97	Celtic	26	12
Total		89	23

CELTIC LEAGUE DEBUT
17 August 1996 v Raith Rovers

ITALY DEBUT
N/A

ITALY HONOURS
None

DID YOU KNOW?
Supersub Paolo started only four games of his 22 appearances at Milan during 1995-96.

Celtic manager Tommy Burns knew he was taking a chance when bringing volatile Italian maestro Paolo Di Canio to Scotland from Serie A giants AC Milan in the summer of 1996. Stark's Park on a freezing Tuesday night in February is a far cry from the San Siro Stadium where the stylish winger shone, after spells with home-town club Lazio and Napoli.

However, the Parkhead faithful did not have long to wait before sampling the two sides of the character who was to both thrill and infuriate them in the season that lay ahead. Delightful touches of skill, seldom seen from any Celt since the heady days of the late 1960s and early 1970s, were interspersed with bouts of petulance which he clearly believed would endear him to the home support.

The gamble paid off in a big way and he immediately became a hero of the Green and White Army who recognised that, if his temperament could be harnessed by Burns, he might just be the man to bring the glory days back to Parkhead.

Di Canio, born in Rome in July 1968, took to life in Scotland like a duck to water, and his off-field contentment was mirrored on the park with a string of breathtaking displays which had journalists struggling to find new superlatives. But as with all geniuses, the magic came at a price. A short temper found him constantly in hot water with officials, but the two red cards and countless yellows he received only served to heighten his appeal with the fans.

The Players' Player of the Year award was testament to the regard in which he was held by his peers, but an end-of-season bust-up with chairman Fergus McCann (which resulted in the Italian being fined two weeks wages) coupled with his failure to turn up for pre-season training cast a huge shadow over his future with the club.

'The dashing Italian is the sort of player
fans drool over.'
GOAL MAGAZINE

1970-1977

Kenny Dalglish

PERSONAL FILE

Born: 4 March 1951
Birthplace: Glasgow
Height: 5' 8"
Weight: 11st 13lb

LEAGUE RECORD

FROM-TO	CLUB	APPS	GOALS
1970-77	Celtic	204	112
1977-90	Liverpool	355	118
Total		559	230

CELTIC LEAGUE DEBUT

4 October 1969 v Raith Rovers

SCOTLAND DEBUT

10 November 1971 v Belgium

SCOTLAND HONOURS

SEASON	CAPS
1971-72	2
1972-73	8
1973-74	12
1974-75	9
1975-76	6
1976-77	10
1977-78	10
1978-79	8
1979-80	10
1980-81	3
1981-82	10
1982-83	2
1983-84	3
1984-85	4
1985-86	3
1986-87	2
Total	102

DID YOU KNOW?

After the 1977 Scottish Cup Final, both Kenny and Jock Stein nearly got on the Rangers bus by mistake...with the trophy!

Sean Fallon's power of persuasion was severely tested before he left the Dalglish home in the south side of Glasgow with the signature of a young man who was to become one of the greatest Celts of all time. The legendary first meeting between Jock Stein's assistant and Dalglish is etched in Celtic folklore – leaving his wife waiting in the car outside for 'a wee minute', Fallon returned some two-and-a-half hours later with the lifelong Rangers fan's signature.

Kenny Dalglish was the complete player. With a lightning-quick brain, his natural strength, mobility and eye for goal made him the most feared predator of his generation. He joined Celtic in 1967 as a 16-year-old. From the start of the 1971-72 season he became a first-team regular, scoring three times in as many games against Rangers (twice in the League Cup) before the campaign was even six weeks old.

Despite a return of more than one goal in every two games, 166 in 320 appearances, Dalglish was never regarded as an out-and-out striker. He was often used by Jock Stein as a link-man just behind the lethal pairing of 'Dixie' Deans and Bobby Lennox.

For some reason Kenny's club form was rarely seen while sporting the dark blue of Scotland and, despite holding a record 102 caps, the first gained against Belgium in November 1971, few outstanding performances readily spring to mind.

Four League Championships and four Scottish Cups had been won before he moved to Liverpool for £440,000 as a direct replacement for Hamburg-bound Kevin Keegan in August 1977. A glittering career littered with countless honours followed at Anfield, as first player and then manager. After taking a well-earned – and much-needed – break from the game, Kenny joined Blackburn, whom he led to the Premiership title in 1995. He currently manages Newcastle United.

Kenny Dalglish rightly lays claim to membership of the 'all-time great Celts' club', due in no small part to the persistence of Mr Fallon and the understanding and patience of his good lady wife.

'He always seemed so positive, even at 15,
    it was inevitable he'd become a good player.'
BILLY McNEILL

1944-1960

Bobby Evans

PERSONAL FILE

Born: 16 July 1927
Birthplace: Glasgow
Height: 5' 8"
Weight: 12st 0lb

LEAGUE RECORD

FROM-TO	CLUB	APPS	GOALS
1944-60	Celtic	385	10
1960-61	Chelsea	32	—
1961-62	Newport Co	31	—
1962-63	Morton	n/k	n/k
1963-65	Third Lanark	n/k	n/k
1965-67	Raith R	n/k	n/k
Total		448	10

CELTIC LEAGUE DEBUT

21 August 1946 v Hearts

SCOTLAND DEBUT

23 October 1948 v Wales

SCOTLAND HONOURS

SEASON	CAPS
1948-49	4
1949-50	4
1950-51	2
1951-52	1
1952-53	1
1953-54	5
1954-55	5
1955-56	4
1956-57	2
1957-58	9
1958-59	4
1959-60	7
Total	48

DID YOU KNOW?

Bobby was voted Scotland's Player of the Year in 1953, and is the third most-capped Celt.

Signed from St Anthony's in 1944, Bobby Evans was the original model of the now-fashionable wing-back. The powerful little redhead was the type of player which every manager wanted in his side. Strong and with energy to burn, Evans was perfect for the role – keen but scrupulously fair in the tackle, powerful in the air, a wonderful reader of the game and with the enthusiasm of a youngster.

Within a few months of breaking into the first team, Evans had made his mark on the international scene. Following a victorious debut against Wales in Cardiff, he inspired his country to a thrilling 3–2 win over Ireland after being two goals down at Hampden in 1948. Evans was capped a further 46 times for Scotland and was honoured by 25 appearances for the old-style Scottish League team. Towards the end of his international career, Evans took over the captaincy of Scotland – a job he retained with supreme confidence.

He moved to a central defensive berth late in his Parkhead career, but even with Billy McNeill in the wings fans were shocked when, in May 1960, Evans was suddenly transferred to Chelsea for a fee of £12,000. After his Celtic days, however, his career went into decline. Moves to Newport County (as player-manager), Morton, Third Lanark and Raith Rovers were relatively unsuccessful.

Evans will always be remembered as a Celtic great. At his best, he was a magnificent and courageous player for the club in a career which spanned over 500 matches in the green-and-white.

Tommy Gemmell

PERSONAL FILE

Born: 16 October 1943
Birthplace: Craigneuk
Height: 6' 2"
Weight: 13st 10lb

LEAGUE RECORD

FROM-TO	CLUB	APPS	GOALS
1961-71	Celtic	247	37
1971-73	Nott'm Forest	39	6
1973-76	Dundee	n/k	n/k
Total		286	43

CELTIC LEAGUE DEBUT
5 January 1963 v Aberdeen

SCOTLAND DEBUT
2 April 1966 v England

SCOTLAND HONOURS

SEASON	CAPS
1965-66	1
1966-67	4
1867-68	2
1968-69	7
1969-70	3
1970-71	1
Total	18

STAR QUOTE
'I took penalties like a golf shot. I pictured the target and made sure I hit it.'

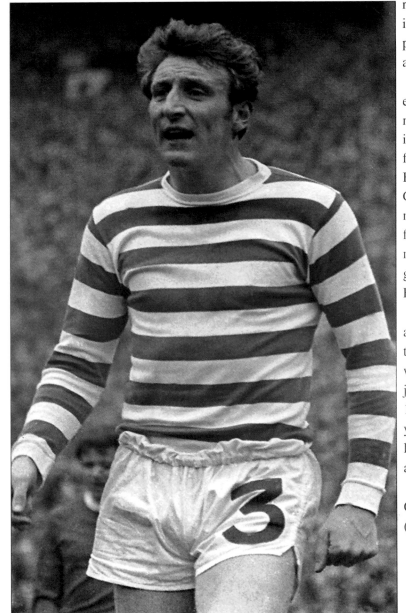

Tommy Gemmell was probably the best defender ever to wear the distinctive hoops of Celtic, but first and foremost he was an entertainer. A flamboyant full-back with a thunderous shot in either foot, 'Big Tam' was idolised by the Parkhead fans…and he knew it.

Gemmell, who had the distinction of scoring in two European Cup Finals, joined Celtic from Coltness United in 1961. Although always remembered for his high-speed forays into the opposing box, he was also an excellent defender who could be relied upon to hold the line in any backs-to-the-wall situation.

Along with skipper Billy McNeill, Tommy chose the return leg of the 1967 European Cup Semi-Final against Dukla Prague to register one of his finest performances for the club in a battling 0-0 draw which saw Celtic advance to the Final.

A tremendous long-range shot helped Gemmell score 64 goals in 418 appearances. A remarkable 31 of them came from penalties, a task Big Tam relished: 'Just make sure you keep it under the crossbar' was a philosophy which paid off for him all but three times in ten years.

Tommy did not always see eye-to-eye with Jock Stein, but neither man allowed this to interfere with the business of filling the Parkhead trophy room. By his own admission, though, Gemmell risked the 'rollicking of my life' when he followed fellow full-back Jim Craig upfield, in the move that led to his unforgettable goal in the 1967 European Cup Final victory over Inter Milan.

Gemmell, who also scored against Feyenoord in a 2-1 defeat three years later in the San Siro, won 18 caps for Scotland before joining Nottingham Forest in 1971. He returned to Dundee two years later, after a spell in Miami, leading them to League Cup glory against Celtic in December 1973.

On retiring in December 1976, Gemmell managed Dundee (1977-80) and Albion Rovers.

Peter Grant

PERSONAL FILE

Born: 30 August 1965
Birthplace: Bellshill
Height: 5' 10"
Weight: 11st 4lb

LEAGUE RECORD

FROM-TO	CLUB	APPS	GOALS
1982-97	Celtic	363	15

CELTIC LEAGUE DEBUT

21 April 1984 v Rangers

SCOTLAND DEBUT

27 May 1989 v England

SCOTLAND HONOURS

SEASON	CAPS
1988-89	2
Total	2

STAR QUOTE

'You can't buy what Peter Grant offers this club.'
TOMMY BURNS

The over-used phrase 'playing for the jersey' could have been penned for Peter Grant, a dedicated one-club man who has served with great distinction since 1982. A whole-hearted midfielder who plays every match as if it is his last, Grant has represented Celtic since being elevated from the Parkhead Boys' Club by manager Billy McNeill after a five-year apprenticeship.

While not exactly shunning the limelight, Grant was more than willing to allow celebrated 'stars' like John Collins and Paul McStay to take the plaudits while going about the business of containing the opposition with a succession of bone-shaking tackles and precision distribution.

Although sometimes unjustly labelled a workhorse, Grant's contribution to the club has never been questioned. He was even willing to sign 14 month-to-month contracts to stay at Parkhead before being offered a new three-year deal in 1993.

An ankle injury kept Grant out of the 1988 Scottish Cup Final success over Dundee United, but he was back at Hampden the following year to collect his first winner's medal in a 1-0 victory over Rangers, a badge he was to add to six years later when Celtic beat Airdrie by a similar score.

When former team-mate Tommy Burns returned to Parkhead as manager in 1995, he moved quickly to ensure that Grant, who also possesses two Championship medals and two caps for Scotland, was not lost to Celtic.

Early in 1997, Grant was rewarded with a testimonial against German giants Bayern Munich and, despite a bitterly cold night in Glasgow where the temperatures barely touched freezing, almost 40,000 fans filled Parkhead to show their appreciation for his dedicated service to the club for which they shared his love.

1965-1974

David Hay

PERSONAL FILE

Born: 29 January 1948
Birthplace: Paisley
Height: 5' 11"
Weight: 11st 7lb

LEAGUE RECORD

FROM-TO	CLUB	APPS	GOALS
1965-74	Celtic	130	6
1974-79	Chelsea	108	2
Total		238	8

CELTIC LEAGUE DEBUT

6 March 1968 v Aberdeen

SCOTLAND DEBUT

18 April 1970 v Northern Ireland

SCOTLAND HONOURS

SEASON	CAPS
1969-70	3
1970-71	5
1971-72	3
1972-73	5
1973-74	11
Total	27

DID YOU KNOW?

Hay was plagued by injury during his time at Chelsea and was forced to endure five operations, including two on his eyes.

Davie Hay can be regarded as one of the greats who have graced the hoops over the years. Hay signed for Celtic in 1966 and was one of the so-called 'Quality Street Kids' – the name given to a Celtic reserve side that included the likes of Kenny Dalglish, Lou Macari and Danny McGrain – who would eventually fill the places left by the ageing Lisbon Lions.

He broke into the first team playing right-back and made an instant impression with his speedy overlaps and his eagerness to get involved in the action. Hay was then moved up to midfield by manager Jock Stein and made his mark there too: indeed, he was soon capped in the position by Scotland manager Tommy Docherty, who gave him the label of the Quiet Assassin. He starred for Scotland in the World Cup of 1974 in Germany before a contract dispute with Celtic resulted in his being transferred to Chelsea.

Hay stayed in the game after his retirement in 1979 and moved into management as boss of Motherwell. He became Celtic supremo in 1983 in succession to Billy McNeill and stayed for four seasons, which yielded the Scottish Cup in 1985 and a dramatic last day League Championship triumph in 1986 when a 5–0 victory against St Mirren handed his team the title after Hearts had lost at Dundee.

Hay was fired in 1987 to make way for the return of Billy McNeill, but came back to Parkhead himself in 1994 as chief scout under Tommy Burns.

Harry Hood

PERSONAL FILE

Born: 3 October 1944
Birthplace: Glasgow
Height: 5' 10"
Weight: 11st 0lb

LEAGUE RECORD

FROM-TO	CLUB	APPS	GOALS
1961-62	Queen's Park	n/k	n/k
1962-64	Clyde	n/k	n/k
1964-66	Sunderland	31	9
1966-69	Clyde	n/k	n/k
1969-76	Celtic	189	74
1976	San Antonio	20	10
1976-77	Motherwell	n/k	n/k
1977-78	Queen of the South	n/k	n/k
Total		240	93

CELTIC LEAGUE DEBUT
29 March 1969 v St Mirren

SCOTLAND DEBUT
N/A

SCOTLAND HONOURS
None

DID YOU KNOW?
While playing for San Antonio Thunder in 1976, Harry played alongside England World Cup winner Bobby Moore.

Harry Hood was always destined to turn out in the green and white of Celtic, but the reason he had to wait until he was approaching his 25th birthday before pulling on the hoops will always remain a mystery. Glasgow-born Hood was frequently linked with a move to Parkhead before he arrived in a £40,000 deal from Clyde in March 1969, after a short spell playing alongside 'Slim' Jim Baxter at Sunderland.

Hood, a lifelong Celtic fan, was a Jock Stein-type player, a beautifully balanced artist blessed with superb close control. Add to this an unerring knack of scoring against Rangers, and it is not hard to see why he became an instant hit with the fans. Harry tasted defeat against the Auld Enemy in one of his very first games for the club, although he did manage the counter in a 2-1 reverse. But the following month, in October 1969, he grabbed the only goal of a stormy match and, as far as the fans were concerned, this was the moment he became one of them.

No player at the time, not even Jimmy Johnstone or Billy McNeill, had the ability to goad the Jungle into full voice quite like Harry, who went on to score 123 goals in 312 appearances (including Cup ties) for the club. A stunning bullet header in the second round of the 1969-70 European Cup campaign against Benfica enhanced his love affair with the supporters, and, after scoring the winner against Rangers in the 1971 Scottish Cup Final replay, the chant of 'Harry, Harry' echoed around Hampden long after the 100,000-plus crowd had departed.

Harry, who again had Rangers on the run when grabbing all three in a 3-1 League Cup semi-final victory in December 1973, won five League Championship medals, three Scottish Cups and two League Cup medals but, incredibly, was never capped at full international level.

Hood was freed in April 1976 and, after unsuccessful spells in management at Albion Rovers and Queen of the South, quit the game to concentrate on his successful business.

John Hughes

LEAGUE RECORD

FROM-TO	CLUB	APPS	GOALS
1959-71	Celtic	255	116
1971-73	Crystal Palace	20	4
1973	Sunderland	1	—
Total		276	120

CELTIC LEAGUE DEBUT
24 August 1960 v Kilmarnock

SCOTLAND DEBUT
8 May 1965 v Spain

SCOTLAND HONOURS

SEASON	CAPS
1964-65	2
1965-66	3
1966-67	—
1967-68	1
1968-69	1
1969-70	1
Total	8

STAR QUOTE

'I've never seen anyone give Jack Charlton a roasting the way Hughes did...he'll do for me.'
DON REVIE

John 'Yogi' Hughes had the annoying ability to infuriate and delight Celtic fans on a minute-to-minute basis. The burly striker was described as powerful and frightening one week, slow and cumbersome the next, and came in for more than his fair share of barracking from impatient terrace-goers. However, Hughes' commitment and popularity as a Celt can never be called into question.

He arrived on the scene as a fearless 17-year-old and, within two weeks of scoring against Third Lanark in the League Cup, Hughes had gained the respect of the hard-to-please Parkhead terrace purists. The hitman again turned on the style seven days later to score in a classic 3–2 win over Rangers at Ibrox.

From that moment on, Hughes carried a weight of expectation on his broad shoulders. It was too much to ask for a player of such little experience to keep up those high standards, but he still grabbed League 116 goals for Celtic – only eight Celts have scored more.

The striker won six Championship medals during the nine-in-a-row run and notched some memorable efforts during that time. Most famous of all was a glorious, glancing header which sank Leeds United in the European Cup Semi-Final of 1970.

Two penalty-kick conversions in the 1965 League Cup Final over Rangers were also a highlight in a career which yielded eight Scotland caps. He played out his career south of the border with Crystal Palace and, briefly, Sunderland.

Mo Johnston

PERSONAL FILE

Born: 13 April 1963
Birthplace: Glasgow
Height: 5' 9"
Weight: 10st 7lb

LEAGUE RECORD

FROM-TO	CLUB	APPS	GOALS
1980-83	Partick Thistle	85	41
1983-84	Watford	38	23
1984-87	Celtic	99	52
1987-89	Nantes	66	22
1989-91	Rangers	76	30
1991-93	Everton	34	10
1993-95	Hearts	35	5
1995-96	Falkirk	41	6
Total		474	189

CELTIC LEAGUE DEBUT

13 October 1984 v Hibernian

SCOTLAND DEBUT

28 February 1984 v Wales

SCOTLAND HONOURS

SEASON	CAPS
1983-84	3
1984-85	5
1985-86	1
1986-87	4
1987-88	7
1988-89	8
1989-90	8
1990-91	—
1991-92	2
Total	38

DID YOU KNOW?
His £400,000 fee when transferred to Celtic was then a Scottish record.

If Maurice Johnston had shot Archduke Ferdinand himself, he could not have caused a bigger furore than he did when becoming the first known Roman Catholic to sign for Rangers in the summer of 1989. 'Celtic are the only team I ever wanted to play for,' he said after being paraded in the club's shirt by manager Billy McNeill, who had brought him 'home' from a three-year exile in France.

However, within days, 'Mojo' had defected to the other side of the city, much to the disgust of the Parkhead faithful, half the Rangers fans and, if former skipper Terry Butcher is to be believed, a good few of the staff at Ibrox as well.

'When he was introduced on a tour of Italy, all the English players made him feel at home,' said Butcher. 'But he wasn't accepted by the Scottish lads at all and even our kit man would not lay out his kit for training.' Whether Johnston knew the consequences of his actions is debatable, but what is not in question is his bravery.

Born in Glasgow in April 1963, Johnston had all the attributes of a truly world-class striker: pace, vision, strength; he was good in the air, and particularly sharp in and around the six-yard box.

Johnston moved to Watford from Partick Thistle in 1983, but – after one free-scoring year down south with Graham Taylor's Watford – Celtic paid £400,000 for his services. He scored an incredible 71 goals in 127 games in all competitions for Celtic before trying his luck in Europe, but after his return to Glasgow became something of a journeyman, with spells at Everton, Hearts and Falkirk and Kansas City Wiz.

Jimmy Johnstone

PERSONAL FILE

Born: 30 September 1944
Birthplace: Glasgow
Height: 5' 4"
Weight: 9st 8lb

LEAGUE RECORD

FROM-TO	CLUB	APPS	GOALS
1961-75	Celtic	308	82
1975	San Jose	10	—
1975-77	Sheffield Utd	11	2
1977	Dundee	n/k	n/k
Total		329	84

CELTIC LEAGUE DEBUT

27 March 1963 v Kilmarnock

SCOTLAND DEBUT

3 October 1964 v Wales

SCOTLAND HONOURS

SEASON	CAPS
1964-65	2
1965-66	1
1966-67	2
1967-68	1
1968-69	2
1969-70	2
1970-71	2
1971-72	5
1972-73	—
1973-74	4
1974-75	2
Total	23

DID YOU KNOW?

Johnstone was selected by France-Football's poll of sports writers to play for the 1967 Earth team against the Universe.

Jimmy Johnstone is, without doubt, the greatest winger ever produced in Scotland. Many will argue a case for Alan Morton, Willie Henderson or even Charlie Cooke, but when on form Johnstone had no equals. 'Jinky' was capable of leaving entire opposing defences in shreds with his close ball control and trademark mazy runs. And, unlike many contemporaries, a fine cross or pinpoint cut-back was usually the culmination of his efforts.

Johnstone had been a ball-boy at Parkhead at the age of 13, before joining the full-time staff in November 1961. He starred for Celtic on countless

occasions – the League decider against Rangers when he scored both goals in the Ibrox mudbath of May 1967, the torment of Leeds' Terry Cooper in the Semi-Final of the 1970 European Cup and, in the dark blue of Scotland, the 2-0 victory over England at Hampden three months before the 1974 World Cup Finals.

But in the eyes of many Celtic fans, the night Jinky really turned it on was against Red Star Belgrade in November 1968. Drawing 1-1 at half-time, Jock Stein told Johnstone, who hated flying, that he would not have to travel to Belgrade for the second leg if the team gained a big enough lead. He went on to run riot in the second half, scoring twice and setting up another two in an unforgettable 5-1 victory.

Although the volatile Johnstone won nine League Championships, five Scottish Cups and five League Cups, he was often in hot water with Stein, who was on record as saying that no player had ever given him as much trouble during his time as a manager. But Johnstone, who won 25 caps for Scotland, also provided Stein with some of his finest moments, notably in the 1967 European Cup Final when the Flying Flea (so-called by Inter Milan boss Helenio Herrera), ran the Italians' rearguard into the ground.

Jimmy left Celtic for San Jose Earthquakes in 1975 and, after short spells at Sheffield United and Dundee among others, returned to Parkhead as a coach under manager David Hay.

Bobby Lennox

PERSONAL FILE

Born: 30 August 1943
Birthplace: Saltcoats
Height: 5' 8"
Weight: 11st 7lb

LEAGUE RECORD

FROM-TO	CLUB	APPS	GOALS
1962-80	Celtic	335	167

CELTIC LEAGUE DEBUT

3 March 1962 v Dundee

SCOTLAND DEBUT

16 November 1966 v Northern Ireland

SCOTLAND HONOURS

SEASON	CAPS
1966-67	3
1967-68	2
1968-69	4
1969-70	1
Total	10

DID YOU KNOW?

*Bobby's nickname 'Lemon' arose
from a newspaper misprint.*

Bobby Charlton once said of Bobby Lennox, 'If I had him on my side I could have played forever…he had it all.' High praise from one who should know, but far from misplaced for a striker whose devastating speed and unerring eye for goal terrorised the best defences at home and abroad throughout the 1960s and 1970s.

Born in Saltcoats, Ayrshire, in August 1943, Bobby was the only Lisbon Lion not born within 30 miles of Glasgow. Lennox was far from fulfilling his potential at Parkhead before the arrival of Jock Stein, who moved him from an out-and-out left-winger into the middle of the park alongside Steve Chalmers.

The switch worked wonders for 'Lemon', who, thriving on an endless supply of ammunition from Bobby Murdoch and Bertie Auld, went on to set a post-war scoring record for the club of 273 goals in 571 appearances in all competitions.

Lennox, like captain Billy McNeill, had the knack of scoring vital goals, notably his last-minute efforts in the League deciders of 1966 and 1968, but it is a disallowed effort in the Semi-Final of the 1966 European Cup Winners' Cup against Liverpool that still haunts him to this day. 'I could not possibly have been offside. I ran past two of their players,' he pleaded after the 2-0 defeat. 'They had their heads in their hands knowing we were through to the Final.'

Lennox, who was capped ten times for Scotland and won 11 League Championships, eight Scottish Cups (the last as a substitute against Rangers in May 1980) and six League Cup medals, enjoyed one of his best games for the club in the 1967 European Cup Final victory over Inter Milan.

In May 1974, Bobby Charlton finally got his chance to play alongside the 'Buzz Bomb' when he pulled on the hoops for Ron Yeats' testimonial at Anfield, a match the Celts won 4-1.

'My job was to
    look for space and run.'

Lou Macari

PERSONAL FILE

Born: 4 June 1949
Birthplace: Edinburgh
Height: 5' 6"
Weight: 10st 10lb

LEAGUE RECORD

FROM-TO	CLUB	APPS	GOALS
1966-73	Celtic	58	27
1973-84	Manchester Utd	329	78
1984-86	Swindon T	36	3
Total		423	108

CELTIC LEAGUE DEBUT

30 April 1969 v Dundee

SCOTLAND DEBUT

24 May 1972 v Wales

SCOTLAND HONOURS

SEASON	CAPS
1971-72	5
1972-73	5
1973-74	—
1974-75	5
1975-76	—
1976-77	4
1977-78	5
Total	24

DID YOU KNOW?

Lou Macari celebrated a decade at Manchester United with a testimonial against Celtic in 1984.

A Quality Street gang member of considerable talent, Luigi Macari was the son of an Italian chip-shop owner. He broke into the Celtic team before old pals Kenny Dalglish and Danny McGrain, making his place secure almost immediately when he showed a useful knack of putting the ball in the net.

It was Macari's dramatic winner in the 1971 Scottish Cup Final, after coming on as substitute for Willie Wallace, which edged out Rangers in a 2-1 win and put him on the Scottish football map. His all-action style, snapping at defenders' heels, was eye-catching, and Scotland honours followed quickly.

He would surely have gone on to even greater things with Celtic but for a falling out with Jock Stein over money – this while he was midway through a five-year contract. In the end, he left the club in early 1973 to join Manchester United for a then-Scottish record £200,000 transfer fee – and, coincidentally or otherwise, the club's era of success was about to draw to a close. Macari had won two Championship and Scottish Cup medals, and appeared in three successive League Cup Finals.

Macari was never one to shy away from publicity, and he was eventually banned from the Scotland side after a night out with five other team-mates while on World Cup duty in Copenhagen.

After a successful career at Old Trafford, he began a rollercoaster managerial career which saw him in trouble with the FA while at Swindon for his alleged involvement in a betting scandal. After spells with West Ham, Birmingham and Stoke, Macari came back to his roots in 1993 when he stepped into Liam Brady's shoes to become Celtic manager. But despite a 2-1 Old Firm win in his first game in charge, things did not go well and he was sacked by Fergus McCann, who claimed he didn't fulfil his managerial duties.

*'If any other Scots club had asked me to
be their manager, I'd still be at Stoke.'*

Frank McAvennie

PERSONAL FILE

Born: 22 November 1959
Birthplace: Glasgow
Height: 5' 10"
Weight: 11st 0lb

LEAGUE RECORD

FROM-TO	CLUB	APPS	GOALS
1980-85	St Mirren	135	50
1985-87	West Ham Utd	85	33
1987-89	Celtic	55	27
1989-92	West Ham Utd	68	16
1992-93	Aston Villa	3	—
1992-93	Celtic	19	9
1993-94	Swindon T (loan)	7	—
1994	Falkirk	3	2
Total		375	137

CELTIC LEAGUE DEBUT
3 October 1987 v Hibernian

SCOTLAND DEBUT
20 November 1985 v Australia

SCOTLAND HONOURS

SEASON	CAPS
1985-86	4
1986-87	—
1987-88	1
Total	5

DID YOU KNOW?
Two of his five Scottish caps were won against the same opponents – Australia.

Frank McAvennie tasted the highs and lows of Scottish football in equal measure during a turbulent two-year stay at Parkhead, which saw him summoned to court following an Old Firm bust-up just 15 days into his Celtic career.

Macca, a prolific goalscorer often likened to Denis Law, joined Celtic for a then record £750,000 from West Ham, and carved a niche for himself in the club's history books when scoring both goals in the 2-1 Scottish Cup Final victory over Dundee United at the end of the team's Centenary year of 1988.

Despite boasting a record of almost one goal in every two games (McAvennie scored 49 in 105 appearances), it is for his part in the Ibrox fracas of 15 October 1987 that he will always be remembered.

Along with Rangers pair Chris Woods and Terry Butcher, McAvennie was shown the red card after a goalmouth scuffle which ended with the Ibrox men being charged with disorderly conduct and fined £500 and £250 respectively.

As expected, McAvennie was found not guilty. The verdict appeared to lift a huge burden from his shoulders and allowed him to resume his prolific goalscoring partnership with Andy Walker, which helped deliver the League and Cup Double later that year.

Frank returned to West Ham for personal reasons the following year, much to the annoyance of the Celtic fans, but never recaptured the goalscoring touch which had tempted the Londoners to part with over £1 million.

Macca was freed three years later and, after unsuccessful short-term spells with Aston Villa, Cliftonville and South China of Hong Kong, he returned to Celtic at the end of 1992, topping up his Parkhead tally by a further nine goals, before departing for good in February 1993.

Several trial periods around the lower divisions were the final stops on his 14-year career: in 1994 he brought the final curtain down on his footballing career, in order to pursue his business interests.

Brian McClair

PERSONAL FILE

Born: 8 December 1963
Birthplace: Bellshill
Height: 5' 10"
Weight: 12st 12lb

LEAGUE RECORD

FROM-TO	CLUB	APPS	GOALS
1980-81	Aston Villa	—	—
1981-83	Motherwell	39	15
1983-87	Celtic	145	99
1987-97	Manchester Utd	342	88
Total		526	202

CELTIC LEAGUE DEBUT

17 September 1983 v Motherwell

SCOTLAND DEBUT

12 November 1986 v Luxembourg

SCOTLAND HONOURS

SEASON	CAPS
1986-87	4
1987-88	3
1988-89	5
1989-90	2
1990-91	3
1991-92	9
1992-93	4
Total	30

DID YOU KNOW?

Unbelievably, at the time Brian signed for Celtic, he was still a Glasgow University student!

Brian McClair will go down in history as one of the most whole-hearted players who have ever played for Celtic. He was actually on Aston Villa's books as a youngster but never made it at Villa Park and returned north of the border to sign for Motherwell. The striker grabbed the headlines in one astonishing week in 1982 when he scored a hat-trick against Rangers and two goals against Celtic for the Fir Park side.

That was more than enough to convince Billy McNeill to sign McClair, and he went on to enjoy a profitable time at Parkhead – even though, ironically, it would be under McNeill's replacement David Hay. 'Choccy' netted 23 goals in 35 League games, bringing an instant return on Celtic's investment. Two goals on the last day of the 1985-86 season helped secure a memorable 5–0 victory over St Mirren which, with once-runaway leaders Hearts capitulating at Dundee, helped give Celtic an unlikely League Championship triumph.

McClair was top scorer for each of his four seasons at Parkhead, netting 35 goals in his final campaign. But former Aberdeen manager Alex Ferguson knew what McClair could do and took him to Old Trafford in a hotly contested transfer deal in which a tribunal eventually awarded Celtic £850,000. He went on to become the first player to score 20 goals in a season for United since George Best and helped his new club claim a host of trophies, including four Premier League titles in five years.

George McCluskey

PERSONAL FILE

Born: 19 September 1957
Birthplace: Hamilton
Height: 5' 11"
Weight: 12st 1lb

LEAGUE RECORD

FROM-TO	CLUB	APPS	GOALS
1974-83	Celtic	145	54
1983-86	Leeds Utd	73	16
1986-89	Hibernian	82	16
1989-92	Hamilton Acad	95	34
1992-94	Kilmarnock	57	13
1994-96	Clyde	35	8
Total		487	141

CELTIC LEAGUE DEBUT

1 November 1975 v Rangers

SCOTLAND DEBUT

N/A

SCOTLAND HONOURS

None (Under-21 only)

DID YOU KNOW?

George scored on his Celtic debut, coming on as sub against Switzerland's FC Valur in October 1975.

If George McKinlay Cassidy McCluskey could have found another yard of pace, he would have been one of the greatest strikers in the history of Celtic. He certainly looked the part when he burst onto the scene in 1979, a product of the Parkhead youth scheme.

He won a Championship medal that season when he helped himself to a dozen goals, and the following year he managed to create a bit of history; it was McCluskey's extra-time winner in the Old Firm Scottish Cup Final which sparked off an on-field riot between rival fans, and, in the aftermath, alcohol was banned from football grounds in Scotland.

McCluskey's career should have blossomed after that, but the emergence of Charlie Nicholas and the prolific goalscoring of Frank McGarvey meant he was left on the bench more often than not. He still managed to score a lot of goals for the hoops until he left for Leeds United in 1983, having decided that manager McNeill preferred the teaming of McGarvey and Nicholas.

His Scotland career never got off the ground, despite being selected by Jock Stein for the Scotland 1982 World Cup squad. When it was trimmed from 40 to the final 22, McCluskey, along with team-mate Tommy Burns, found himself out in the cold. At club level, though, his goals helped Celtic to three titles in five seasons.

It is unfortunate that a player with such an abundance of skill could not fulfil his total potential during nearly a decade at Parkhead, but McCluskey enjoyed a long career playing well into his thirties with Kilmarnock and Clyde.

'I wanted George to show me why he should be in the team every week.'
BILLY McNEILL

Frank McGarvey

STAR QUOTE
'I wouldn't like to have played against him!'
JOCK STEIN

Francis Peter McGarvey's most famous moment as a Celtic player went hand in hand with his biggest disappointment. The unpredictable striker left Celtic Park just days after helping the club to one of its most famous triumphs.

McGarvey stooped to head a dramatic late winner, which secured a 2–1 win over Dundee United in the Centenary 1985 Scottish Cup Final. It remains a priceless moment in the memory of most Celtic fans, yet McGarvey's reward was a poor contract offer for the following season and a subsequent £75,000 transfer to St Mirren.

Having started his League career with a bang at St Mirren under Alex Ferguson's tutelage, McGarvey was signed from Liverpool reserves by Billy McNeill. The price was a club record £250,000 in March 1980, and Frank accepted a drop in wages to ensure first-team football. His partnership with a vibrant teenager by the name of

Charles Nicholas was feared throughout Scotland, 'Prince Charlie's sublime skill being complemented by McGarvey's hard work and a flair for the unexpected. It was suggested that Frank had no idea what his next move on the pitch would be – making it near impossible for his team-mates, let alone the opposition, to figure it out.

However, the fans loved his all-or-nothing style and he rewarded them with a succession of goals and vintage displays. McGarvey scored 78 times in the League for the hoops and collected five medals – League winner in 1981 and 1982, Cup winner in 1980 and 1985, and a 1982 League Cup winner's badge.

Danny McGrain

PERSONAL FILE

Born: 1 May 1950
Birthplace: Finnieston
Height: 5' 9"
Weight: 12st 1lb

LEAGUE RECORD

FROM-TO	CLUB	APPS	GOALS
1967-87	Celtic	439	4
1987-88	Hamilton Acad	21	—
Total		460	4

CELTIC LEAGUE DEBUT

26 August 1970 v Dundee United

SCOTLAND DEBUT

12 May 1973 v Wales

SCOTLAND HONOURS

SEASON	CAPS
1972-73	5
1973-74	10
1974-75	7
1975-76	6
1976-77	10
1977-78	2
1978-79	—
1979-80	7
1980-81	8
1981-82	7
Total	62

STAR QUOTE

'When he tackles you, you stay tackled.'
CHARLIE NICHOLAS

Assistant manager Sean Fallon spotted a young Danny McGrain playing for Scotland schoolboys in 1967, and one look was all he needed to be convinced he had a future star on his hands. Daniel Fergus McGrain, often to be found at Ibrox as a schoolboy (although he insists: 'I was never a real Rangers supporter'), was the mainstay of Jock Stein's Quality Street Kids. The team included Kenny Dalglish, Lou Macari, Davie Hay and George Connelly, and was charged with continuing the trophy-flow as the Lisbon Lions approached their sell-buy date in the early 1970s.

A ferocious tackler, he also possessed devastating speed and vision, and is widely regarded as the greatest right full-back ever to sport the green and white hoops. He played 657 times in all competitions, scoring eight goals, in a glittering Celtic career that saw him pick up five Championship medals, four Scottish Cups and one League Cup.

Yet he was no stranger to serious injury or illness. In 1972 he fractured his skull playing against Falkirk at Brockville, and five years later picked up a foot injury against Hibernian which was so serious it kept him out of the first team for 18 months. In between, in 1974, he was diagnosed as having diabetes, an illness he insisted would not prevent him plying his trade at the very highest level.

McGrain, who won the first of his 62 caps for Scotland against Wales in 1973, was granted a testimonial against Manchester United in 1980 and when his glittering career ended seven years later, fans fully expected his 20 years of dedication to the club to result in a back-room post being offered.

But the silence from the boardroom was deafening, and McGrain, who was awarded the MBE for services to football in 1983, was allowed to leave to join Hamilton Accies, before taking over as coach at Douglas Park, a position he resigned just one year later.

Jimmy McGrory

PERSONAL FILE

Born: 26 April 1904
Birthplace: Garngad
Died: 20 October 1982
Height: 5' 8"
Weight: 11st 8lb

LEAGUE RECORD

FROM-TO	CLUB	APPS	GOALS
1922-37	Celtic	378	397
1923-24	Clydebank (loan)	n/k	n/k
Total		378	397

CELTIC LEAGUE DEBUT

20 January 1923 v Third Lanark

SCOTLAND DEBUT

25 February 1928 v Northern Ireland

SCOTLAND HONOURS

Season	Caps
1927-28	1
1928-29	—
1929-30	—
1930-31	1
1931-32	2
1932-33	2
1933-34	1
Total	7

DID YOU KNOW?
*Celtic would have lost their
greatest player had Bury taken him
on after a trial early in 1921.*

Arguably the greatest Celtic player of them all, this stocky striker was signed from junior side St Roch's, but failed to make an immediate impact and was farmed out to Clydebank in 1923. McGrory used that period to gain confidence and he returned a stronger and better player, hustling defenders into submission. His astonishing record of 397 goals in 378 League games is one that will never be surpassed and remains an achievement almost unmatched in world football.

He scored a total of 550 goals for Celtic and they included some memorable individual scoring feats. He netted eight goals in one match against Dunfermline in 1928, and scored a hat-trick in three minutes against Motherwell eight years later. For a small man, he scored a disproportionate number of goals with his head (becoming known as the Golden Crust) and was incredibly brave.

Dedicated to Celtic, he refused all efforts to transfer him to Arsenal in 1928, and five years later scored the only goal of that year's Cup Final despite suffering two broken teeth in an early collision. Little wonder a statue of the player now has pride of place in the Celtic Park entrance foyer.

McGrory, who'd mysteriously only amassed a total of seven Scotland caps,

became manager of Kilmarnock from 1937 until the Second World War halted football. He was appointed Celtic manager after the war and was 20 years in the job before making way for Jock Stein. McGrory was public relations manager for the club until his death in 1982.

Murdo MacLeod

PERSONAL FILE

Born: 24 September 1958
Birthplace: Glasgow
Height: 5' 9"
Weight: 12st 4lb

LEAGUE RECORD

FROM-TO	CLUB	APPS	GOALS
1974-78	Dumbarton	87	9
1978-87	Celtic	281	55
1987-90	B Dortmund	n/k	n/k
1990-93	Hibernian	78	2
1993-95	Dumbarton	66	1
1995-96	Partick Thistle	1	—
Total		513	67

CELTIC LEAGUE DEBUT
4 November 1978 v Motherwell

SCOTLAND DEBUT
25 May 1985 v England

SCOTLAND HONOURS

SEASON	CAPS
1984-85	1
1985-86	—
1986-87	4
1987-88	2
1988-89	2
1989-90	8
1990-91	3
Total	20

STAR QUOTE
'Murdo's been a hell of a good servant to Celtic.'
BILLY McNEILL

Murdo MacLeod was famous for having one of the hardest shots in Scottish football. When he let go one of his trademark left-foot power drives, it used to strike fear into the hearts of both defenders and goalkeepers.

He made his mark when making his debut for Dumbarton in 1976 and soon attracted the attention of other clubs, but Celtic were first to snap him up. He made the perfect start to his Parkhead career when he scored the goal that wrapped up the League. Celtic needed to beat Rangers in 1979 to win the title and were 2–1 down to their biggest rivals. But backed by a massive home crowd, they stormed into a 3–2 lead before MacLeod unleashed a typically unstoppable 30-yard drive that smashed into the net in the last minute.

The first of 20 Scottish caps came when he came on at Hampden in 1985's Home International with England, replacing Gordon Strachan. His big-match experience served him well as Scotland ran out single-goal winners.

He stayed nine seasons at Parkhead and won every honour in the Scottish game before broadening his horizons with a move to Borussia Dortmund in 1987. MacLeod fitted into the German lifestyle and was a popular player among the Dortmund fans.

He returned to Scotland with Hibs as player-coach before moving to Dumbarton three years later and venturing into management. He guided them to promotion to Division One before accepting the post of Partick Thistle manager, but was fired after two seasons at Firhill.

Billy McNeill

PERSONAL FILE

Born: 2 March 1940
Birthplace: Bellshill
Height: 6' 1"
Weight: 12st 0lb

LEAGUE RECORD

FROM-TO	CLUB	APPS	GOALS
1957-75	Celtic	486	22

CELTIC LEAGUE DEBUT

6 September 1958 v Rangers

SCOTLAND DEBUT

15 April 1961 v England

SCOTLAND HONOURS

Season	Caps
1960-61	4
1961-62	4
1962-63	2
1963-64	3
1964-65	4
1965-66	2
1966-67	1
1967-68	1
1968-69	4
1969-70	1
1970-71	—
1971-72	3
Total	29

DID YOU KNOW?
Rumours were rife in the summer of 1964 that Spurs were prepared to offer Billy a move to London.

62

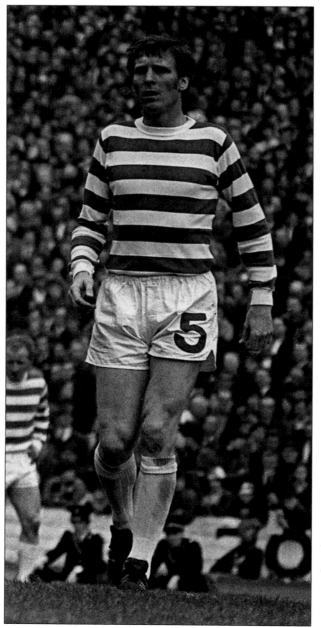

A stunning goal by Billy McNeill in the dying minutes of the 1965 Scottish Cup Final changed a team of perennial losers into the most successful outfit ever produced in the British Isles. When Billy headed Charlie Gallagher's 82nd-minute corner beyond Dunfermline keeper Jim Herriot, he, according to Jock Stein, who had arrived at the club just two months earlier, showed his team-mates how to win.

McNeill went on to become the most successful captain in the club's history, winning every honour the game had to offer, culminating in European Cup glory over Inter Milan in May 1967. He had already won the first of his paltry 29 Scotland caps before Stein arrived, but it was after the Big Man took over that the pair changed the face of Scottish football almost overnight.

A dominant figure who commanded his penalty area like a general, 'Caesar' looked every inch a captain, and his aerial prowess, whether in attack or defence, made him one of the most feared members of the star-studded Celtic team of the day.

Totalling 790 appearances in all, his 16-year Celtic career produced nine successive League Championship, seven Scottish Cup, and six League Cup medals, together with the 1965 Scottish Player of the Year award. But surely his biggest moment must have been on that glorious night in Lisbon when McNeill collected the European Cup winner's badge, finally hanging up his boots after leading Celtic to a Scottish Cup Final victory over Airdrie in May 1975.

McNeill returned to succeed Stein as manager three years later, after spells at Clyde and Aberdeen, leading Celtic to three Premier Division titles and a Scottish Cup success, before being replaced by David Hay after an apparent disagreement with the board.

Unsuccessful spells in charge at Manchester City and Aston Villa followed, before he answered the call to return home to halt the march of the Blue Army which was sweeping all before them under the leadership of Graeme Souness.

Caesar again proved he was the man for the big job, delivering the League and Cup Double in the club's Centenary year of 1988 and the Scottish Cup the following year. However, not for the first time, the Parkhead board showed unbelievable short-sightedness in dismissing him after a two-year trophy 'famine' and replacing him with arguably the most unpopular man ever to fill the manager's hot seat – Liam Brady.

Many a moon will shine over Parkhead before we see Billy McNeill's like again. He is, quite simply, the greatest Celt of all time.

'At the start of the season, the European Cup seemed like an impossible dream.'

John McPhail

PERSONAL FILE

Born: 27 December 1923
Birthplace: Lambhill
Height: 6' 0"
Weight: 13st 7lb

LEAGUE RECORD

FROM-TO	CLUB	APPS	GOALS
1941-56	Celtic	142	54

CELTIC LEAGUE DEBUT
12 April 1947 v Hibernian

SCOTLAND DEBUT
9 November 1949 v Wales

SCOTLAND HONOURS

Season	Caps
1949-50	1
1950-51	3
1951-52	—
1952-53	—
1953-54	1
Total	5

DID YOU KNOW?
Following his retirement, John became a Daily Record *journalist before working for the club newspaper.*

One of the most popular figures of his era with the Celtic support, big John McPhail was signed from Strathclyde Juniors in 1941. Though six feet tall and powerfully built, his great asset was his versatility and he could (and did) play in almost any position. His career was hampered by injury, however, and at one point early in his postwar career he was sent to Ireland to recover from tuberculosis.

Although he began his Parkhead stint as a right-half, where his strength in the tackle was put to best use, he was soon switched to centre-forward in 1950 and became a remarkable success in his new role. He netted with frequent regularity and was an excellent leader on the park, having been appointed captain in summer 1948.

McPhail was a major figure in taking Celtic to their first Scottish Cup triumph for 14 years in 1951, scoring seven of their 19 Cup goals despite missing two rounds through injury. His finest hour was the Final against Motherwell where he scored a memorable winner after 12 minutes, tearing through the centre of the defence before lifting the ball over the stranded keeper.

McPhail won five Scotland caps (the last a surprise recall against Northern Ireland in October 1953), scoring three goals, represented the Scottish League and was part of two Championship-winning teams. Weight problems plagued his later days at Parkhead, and he retired in the summer of 1956 having played nearly 150 League games for his one and only club.

Paul McStay

PERSONAL FILE

Born: 22 October 1964
Birthplace: Hamilton
Height: 5' 10"
Weight: 10st 7lb

LEAGUE RECORD

FROM-TO	CLUB	APPS	GOALS
1981-97	Celtic	514	57

CELTIC LEAGUE DEBUT

30 January 1982 v Aberdeen

SCOTLAND DEBUT

21 September 1983 v Uruguay

SCOTLAND HONOURS

Season	Caps
1983-84	6
1984-85	5
1985-86	4
1986-87	7
1987-88	8
1988-89	8
1989-90	11
1990-91	3
1991-92	8
1992-93	7
1993-94	2
1994-95	3
1995-96	1
1996-97	3
Total	76

DID YOU KNOW?
Paul became Celtic's most capped player on 14 October 1992, overtaking Danny McGrain's 62.

Few who watched Paul McStay orchestrate Scotland schoolboys' 5-4 victory over England at Wembley in 1980 could have doubted that a glittering career at the highest level lay ahead for the modest young man. A gifted midfielder with superb close control and pinpoint distribution, McStay made his debut as a 17-year-old marking his first full game in the hoops with a goal against Aberdeen at Pittodrie.

McStay, who joined Celtic from Parkhead Boys' Club in February 1981, was only 18 when he earned his first cap for Scotland in a 2-0 victory over Uruguay at Hampden. In January 1990 he followed

his Great Uncles, Willie and Jimmy McStay, by becoming the third member of his family to captain Celtic when Roy Aitken was transferred to Newcastle United.

But his tenure as skipper coincided with Rangers' domination of the domestic scene, and the Scottish Cup victory over Airdrie in 1995 was his sole moment of glory while leading the Bhoys.

A one-club man who shunned lucrative offers from top English and European clubs, McStay won three Championship, one League Cup and three Scottish Cup medals in a career which saw him turn out over 600 times for the hoops. Labelled 'unquestionably the best player in Scotland in the late 1980s' by team-mate Tommy Burns, McStay represented his country 76 times – the last as a substitute against Austria at Parkhead in April 1997.

Awarded the MBE for services to football in the 1997 New Years' Honours List, McStay, who was rewarded for his loyalty by Celtic with a lucrative testimonial against Manchester United in 1995, was forced to quit the game due to a persistent ankle injury in May 1997. A quiet, modest family man who never made an enemy on or off the park during his glittering 16-year stay at Parkhead, McStay must surely be acknowledged as one of Celtic's all-time greats.

Gordon Marshall

PERSONAL FILE

Born: 19 April 1964
Birthplace: Edinburgh
Height: 6' 2"
Weight: 12st 0lb

LEAGUE RECORD

FROM-TO	CLUB	APPS	GOALS
1982-83	East Stirling (loan)	15	—
1983-87	East Fife	158	—
1987-91	Falkirk	171	—
1991-97	Celtic	100	—
1993-94	Stoke C (loan)	10	—
Total		454	—

CELTIC LEAGUE DEBUT

23 November 1991 v Airdrieonians

SCOTLAND DEBUT

17 May 1992 v United States

SCOTLAND HONOURS

1991-92	1
Total	1

DID YOU KNOW?

To emphasise his ambitions, Gordon boasted Banks (England's 1966 World Cup keeper) among his Christian names.

Gordon Marshall was clearly born to be a goalkeeper. His father, a Parkhead reserve also named Gordon, played just one competitive game for the Bhoys, a European Cup match in 1971, before moving on to Aberdeen and then Arbroath. Son Gordon would make his debut in Celtic colours exactly 20 years later, having been bought – also as a reserve – by then-manager Liam Brady

This game against Airdrie was his one and only appearance that term when first-choice Republic of Ireland international Packy Bonner was injured. The next season, he made 16 appearances to Bonner's 20, and when Tommy Burns took the hot seat Gordon made his move and became an ever-present.

Marshall had started his career at Ibrox, but a broken leg scuppered hopes of first-team football on that side of Glasgow. East Stirling (loan), East Fife and Falkirk were the beneficiaries, and it was clear he only needed a bigger stage to take the final step to international football. This came when he made the Scotland squad less than a year after his arrival at Parkhead.

Liam Brady invested £275,000 on the advice of his assistant Tommy Craig, realising the importance of having two good goalkeepers. And if the central defenders immediately in front of him, Boyd and Hughes, had helped Celtic boast the best defensive record in the Scottish Premier Division, Marshall had also contributed with numerous shut-outs. His consistency, sure handling ability, quick shot-stopping reflexes and sound positional sense would surely have made him an international regular had it not been for the dependable duo of Leighton and Goram ahead of him in the pecking order.

Tommy Burns' final season at the helm saw him pick Stuart Kerr from the outset but Gordon found his way back to first-team action later in the season when the youngster dislocated a finger. The preferences of the Jock Brown/Wim Jansen pairing had yet to be ascertained at the time of writing, but at 33 Marshall certainly had no need to consider hanging up his gloves just yet.

Tony Mowbray

PERSONAL FILE

Born: 22 November 1963
Birthplace: Saltburn
Height: 6' 2"
Weight: 13st 2lb

LEAGUE RECORD

FROM-TO	CLUB	APPS	GOALS
1981-91	Middlesbrough	348	25
1991-95	Celtic	88	6
1995-97	Ipswich Town	19	2
Total		455	33

CELTIC LEAGUE DEBUT
9 November 1991 v Aberdeen

ENGLAND DEBUT
N/A

ENGLAND HONOURS
None (England B only)

DID YOU KNOW?
Tony Mowbray was born on the very day President Kennedy was assassinated.

He doesn't enjoy the tag, but Tony Mowbray can be described as one of the most unfortunate Celts in the club's glittering history. The rugged Teessider had built up a reputation as a man mountain and a leader of men during a brilliant ten-year career at Middlesbrough. Celtic installed Liam Brady as manager for the 1991 season, and he immediately pinpointed 'Mogga' as the man to strengthen a weak Parkhead defence.

After four months of chasing, Brady finally captured the England B international in November that year in a deal worth £900,000 to Boro. Since the previous month had seen Celtic concede five goals to Swiss team Neuchatel, his appearance was overdue by anyone's standards.

Mowbray announced on his arrival that he was not flashy, preferring to fight, work, lead and win possession before allowing Celtic's ball-players to take charge. It was a theory which won admiration

from the Parkhead faithful, but the reality of Mogga's career in the hoops was somewhat different. In ten years at Boro, Mowbray had never suffered serious injury. Within three weeks at Celtic, he was struck down with a troublesome ankle injury which never properly cleared during his four-year stay.

Mowbray also suffered the pain of tragically losing his wife Bernadette to cancer during his time in Glasgow and his touching story of devotion to her, even after her passing away, won him countless admirers in and out of the game.

Mowbray left Celtic in 1995 in a £350,000 deal which took him to Ipswich, where his career was once again to be ravaged by continuing injuries, but by that time his courage and bravery in adversity had made him a never-to-be-forgotten Celt.

1959-1973

Bobby Murdoch

PERSONAL FILE

Born: 17 August 1944
Birthplace: Bothwell
Height: 5' 11"
Weight: 12st 1lb

LEAGUE RECORD

FROM-TO	CLUB	APPS	GOALS
1959-73	Celtic	291	62
1973-76	Middlesbrough	95	6
Total		386	68

CELTIC LEAGUE DEBUT
8 September 1962 v Rangers

SCOTLAND DEBUT
9 November 1965 v Italy

SCOTLAND HONOURS

SEASON	CAPS
1965-66	4
1966-67	1
1967-68	1
1968-69	5
1969-70	1
Total	12

DID YOU KNOW?
His boyhood hero at Our Lady's High School was First XI captain Billy McNeill.

68

More than any other player, Bobby Murdoch benefited from the arrival of Jock Stein, the manager who moulded him into one of the greatest players ever to wear the green and white of Celtic.

Murdoch had been six years at the club, having little success as an old-fashioned inside-forward when Stein, who took over in 1965, moved him alongside Bertie Auld to form the engine room of the 4-2-4 formation which was to fill the Parkhead trophy room to bursting point over the next decade.

The duo, neither of whom could boast the quickest turn of foot, were given the job of forming a seamless link between the rearguard marshalled by Billy McNeill and the fast-paced front pairing of Steve Chalmers and Bobby Lennox, a task they took to with consummate ease.

Murdoch, who had joined the club straight from school before being 'farmed out' to Cambuslang Rangers, won the first of his 12 Scotland caps against Italy in November 1965, before going on to accumulate eight Scottish League Championship medals, four Scottish Cups and five Scottish League Cups.

Named Scotland's Player of the Year in 1969, he was also a key member of the Lisbon Lions who delivered the European Cup to Parkhead after a 2-1 victory over Inter Milan in May 1967. Jack Charlton described him as 'one of the best players I have ever worked with, and certainly the best I've ever signed,'

when he took him to Middlesbrough after he made his final appearance in the hoops at the start of the 1973-74 season.

Celtic have always produced cultured midfielders: future stars like Davie Hay, Tommy Burns, Paul McStay and John Collins were to continue the tradition, but none were blessed with the sheer physical presence of Murdoch whose successor as a truly world-class, ball-winning playmaker has yet to be introduced to the Parkhead fans.

'His greatest quality is consistency.'
JOCK STEIN

Charlie Nicholas

PERSONAL FILE

Born: 30 December 1961
Birthplace: Glasgow
Height: 5' 10"
Weight: 11st 4lb

LEAGUE RECORD

FROM-TO	CLUB	APPS	GOALS
1979-83	Celtic	159	85
1983-88	Arsenal	151	34
1988-90	Aberdeen	78	30
1990-95	Celtic	28	2
1995-96	Clyde	31	5
Total		447	156

CELTIC LEAGUE DEBUT

16 August 1980 v Kilmarnock

SCOTLAND DEBUT

30 March 1983 v Switzerland

SCOTLAND HONOURS

SEASON	CAPS
1982-83	6
1983-84	2
1984-85	4
1985-86	5
1986-87	2
1987-88	—
1988-89	1
Total	20

DID YOU KNOW?
Nicholas enjoyed the nickname 'Charles de Goal' during his first spell at Parkhead.

Idolised wherever he played, Charlie Nicholas burst onto the Scottish football scene in the 1980-81 season, netting 28 goals in 39 games for Celtic. A prolific goalscorer with superb technical ability who could prise open the meanest defence with one of his trademark flicks, Champagne Charlie joined his boyhood heroes from the Parkhead Boys' Club in June 1979. A spell in the reserves was cut short when top clubs from south of the border began to take an interest in the precocious teenager.

Elevated to the first team, Charlie seized his chance – and six goals in ten appearances were already in the bag when, during the 1981-82 season, he broke his leg playing for the reserves against Morton at Cappielow. However, Charlie returned with a bang the following campaign and an incredible 46-goal haul in 50 matches tempted Arsenal boss Terry Neill to part with £650,000 to take him south to Highbury.

Born in Glasgow in December 1961, Charlie, who quickly became the toast of the North Bank, was not exactly the darling of new boss George Graham and, despite scoring both goals in Arsenal's 1987 League Cup win over Liverpool, was on his way back north to Aberdeen in a £400,000 deal the following year.

However, a Scottish Cup Final victory over Celtic in 1990 was greeted with less than normal enthusiasm, so it was no surprise when he headed north to return to his first love in the summer. He still possessed the ability to turn a game single-handedly but, playing in one of the poorest Celtic sides for years, was unable to add to his collection of medals – two League Championship, three Scottish Cup, one English League Cup and two League Cup – during his four-year stay at Parkhead.

Charlie, who gained 20 caps for Scotland between 1983 and 1989, signed for Clyde in late 1995 before quitting the following season to take up a career in broadcasting, where his expert reading of the game and witty comments make him a sought-after pundit on both TV and radio.

Davie Provan

PERSONAL FILE

Born: 8 May 1956
Birthplace: Gourock
Height: 5' 10"
Weight: 11st 4lb

LEAGUE RECORD

FROM-TO	CLUB	APPS	GOALS
1974-78	Kilmarnock	n/k	n/k
1978-87	Celtic	206	27
Total		206	27

CELTIC LEAGUE DEBUT
23 September 1978 v Partick Thistle

SCOTLAND DEBUT
21 November 1979 v Belgium

SCOTLAND HONOURS

Season	Caps
1979-80	4
1980-81	3
1981-82	3
Total	10

DID YOU KNOW?
Davie was loaned to Sydney Olympic in the summer of 1985.

A moment of pure genius towards the end of the 1985 Scottish Cup Final earned Davie Provan his rightful place in Celtic folklore. 'Only two goals have ever been scored direct from free-kicks in the Scottish Cup Final. Is this history in the making?' were the prophetic utterings of commentator Archie MacPherson who, three seconds later, was describing Hamish McAlpine picking Provan's exquisitely-struck 20-yard curler out of the back of his net.

Frank McGarvey went on to score a last-gasp winner to ensure the trophy returned to Parkhead, but the match will always be remembered for that Davie Provan goal'.

Provan began his senior career with Kilmarnock in May 1974, after a brief stint at junior club Port Glasgow Rovers. An old-fashioned winger in the mould of Lisbon Lion 'Jinky' Johnstone, Provan possessed a lethal shot in either foot and the ability to put the ball on the proverbial 'tanner' from anywhere in the park. Billy McNeill, who had tried to sign him during his time in charge at Aberdeen, paid former Parkhead team-mate Willie Fernie £120,000 for his signature in September 1978, a capture many fans rate as the best signing of the decade.

The move paid instant dividends, and Provan helped deliver the League title later that year when choosing the infamous 4-2 Championship decider against Rangers at Parkhead to produce his best-ever game in the hoops. Two further Championships, a Scottish Cup and a Scottish League Cup followed in the next three years, during which time Provan picked up ten caps for Scotland and was nominated Scottish Player of the Year in 1980.

He went on to make 284 appearances for the club, scoring 42 goals, before being struck down with Myalgic Encephalomyelitis, an energy-sapping illness which ended his career prematurely in 1985. Celtic fans were given one last chance to witness his skill and 40,000 turned up for his swansong in a testimonial match with Nottingham Forest in December 1987. These days, he is recognised as one of the finest TV and radio broadcasters on the game in Scotland.

Ronnie Simpson

PERSONAL FILE

Born: 11 October 1930
Birthplace: Glasgow
Height: 5' 10"
Weight: 11st 13lb

LEAGUE RECORD

FROM-TO	CLUB	APPS	GOALS
1945-49	Queen's Park	n/k	n/k
1951-60	Newcastle Utd	262	—
1960-64	Hibernian	n/k	n/k
1964-70	Celtic	118	—
Total		380	—

CELTIC LEAGUE DEBUT

21 November 1964 v Falkirk

SCOTLAND DEBUT

15 April 1967 v England

SCOTLAND HONOURS

Season	Caps
1966-67	2
1967-68	2
1968-69	1
Total	5

DID YOU KNOW?
Ronnie was loaned to arch rivals Rangers in April 1947, but failed to make a breakthrough into the first-team.

Nine years had elapsed since Ronnie Simpson last tasted glory, and a £4,000 move from Hibernian to Celtic in September 1964 was generally regarded as one last pay-day before the boots were hung up. But the superbly agile stopper was to cram in more awards over the next five years with Celtic than he could have dared imagine when making his debut for Queen's Park still 64 days shy of his 15th birthday.

Moving to Newcastle United following National Service in 1951, he enjoyed a nine-year stay in the English First Division, a stint highlighted by two FA Cup winner's medals, against Arsenal in 1952 and Manchester City three years later, before returning north to Easter Road in October 1960. Simpson's positional sense was immaculate and, despite his relative lack of inches for a keeper, he had little trouble cutting out the most accurate crosses from either wing.

Known as 'Faither' to his younger team-mates, Ronnie played 188 times for Celtic following his debut in November 1964, keeping a remarkable 91 clean sheets – almost one every two games – while

amassing four Championship, one Scottish Cup and three League Cup medals.

Capped for the first time in April 1967 in a 3-2 European Championship victory over World Champions England, a further four were to follow, and Simpson was named Scottish Player of the Year a month later before crowning his glittering career with a European Cup winner's medal with the famous Lisbon Lions.

A shoulder injury forced Simpson to quit the game in 1970, and he missed out on one last bow when, with the League title already won for the sixth successive year, Jock Stein decided to parade the Lions of Lisbon one last time, against Clyde in May 1971.

Jock Stein

PERSONAL FILE

Born: 6 October 1922
Birthplace: Earnock
Died: 10 September 1985
Height: 5' 11"
Weight: 11st 7lb

LEAGUE RECORD

FROM-TO	CLUB	APPS	GOALS
1942-50	Albion Rovers	n/k	n/k
1951-57	Celtic	106	2
Total		106	2

CELTIC LEAGUE DEBUT

8 December 1951 v St Mirren

SCOTLAND DEBUT

N/A

SCOTLAND HONOURS

None

STAR QUOTE
'I was good in the air and could tackle a bit – but nothing special.'

Known throughout the footballing world as 'the Big Man' – a tag he neither sought nor felt at ease with – Jock Stein CBE single-handedly changed the fortunes of Celtic, turning them from the proverbial under-achieving sleeping giants into Champions of Europe. Within two months of his arrival at Parkhead, Stein ended the Bhoys' seven-year trophy famine by guiding them to Scottish Cup glory over Dunfermline, the club where he cut his teeth in management after a spell in charge of Celtic's second string.

By his own admission, Stein could never be regarded as a 'top drawer' player, and the playing career of the former miner from Burnbank, Lanarkshire, was halted by an ankle injury in January 1957.

After what chairman Bob Kelly described as a 'farming out' period at East End Park and Hibernian, Stein returned in March 1965 to take over the reins of Celtic, as only the third manager in their 77-year history.

A period of unprecedented success followed, as the Big Man moulded a bunch of talented individuals from the west of Scotland into one of the most feared attacking teams in Europe which delivered nine successive titles, six Scottish Cups, six Scottish League Cups and the European Cup in 1967, to equal the world record.

'John, you're immortal now,' said Liverpool boss and good friend Bill Shankly, after the 2-1 victory over Inter Milan in Lisbon, a statement no Celtic fan who had suffered through the barren years before his arrival would disagree with.

Stein almost lost his life in an horrific car crash in 1975, but recovered to lead Celtic to the League and Cup Double of 1977 before making way for Billy McNeill a year later. An ill-fated 44-day stint as manager of Leeds followed, before he returned home to take charge of the national side.

He led Scotland to their third successive World Cup Finals in Spain in 1982 and had guided them to within touching distance of Mexico '86 when a fatal heart attack claimed his life at a vital qualifier in Cardiff in September 1985. Stein commanded the respect of players and managers alike, but was never afraid to put a 'star' in his place while finding time to listen to the youngest member of his groundstaff.

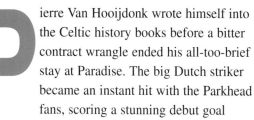

Pierre Van Hooijdonk

PERSONAL FILE

Born: 29 November 1969
Birthplace: Steenbergen, Holland
Height: 6' 4"
Weight: 13st 5lb

LEAGUE RECORD

FROM-TO	CLUB	APPS	GOALS
1994-97	Celtic	69	44
1997	Nott'm Forest	8	1
Total		77	45

CELTIC LEAGUE DEBUT
11 January 1995 v Hearts

HOLLAND DEBUT
14 December 1994 v Luxembourg

HOLLAND HONOURS
Has been capped at Under-21 and full levels by his country

DID YOU KNOW?
During his Dutch club career, Pierre scored 114 goals in 182 games.

Pierre Van Hooijdonk wrote himself into the Celtic history books before a bitter contract wrangle ended his all-too-brief stay at Paradise. The big Dutch striker became an instant hit with the Parkhead fans, scoring a stunning debut goal against Hearts following his £1.2 million move from NAC Breda in January 1995. A lethal dead-ball expert, and, at six foot four, an aerial threat to the best defences, Van Hooijdonk grabbed a further seven goals, including the only strike in the Scottish Cup Final victory over Airdrie, before the season was over.

Van Hooijdonk began his career at Roosendaal before moving to Breda where his goals helped them lift the coveted Dutch Team of the Season award in 1993-94. He took up where he left off the following campaign, becoming the first Celt in almost a decade to find the net over 30 times.

His 32-goal haul helped him earn a call-up for the Dutch side, a chance he grabbed with both hands by scoring twice in a 3-1 World Cup qualifying victory over Wales in Cardiff. Portuguese striker Jorge Cadete arrived from Sporting Lisbon to form the partnership manager Tommy Burns hoped would deliver the League Championship to Parkhead after a nine-year absence.

But the pairing barely had a chance to gel before Van Hooijdonk, upset at his wage level compared to other top players at the club, became involved in a war of words with chairman Fergus McCann. This ended with him moving to English Premiership side Nottingham Forest after reportedly rejecting a £7,000-a-week pay offer. Forest, languishing at the foot of the table, paid £3.5 million for his services, but a return of just one goal in eight games could not help them preserve their top-flight status.

'I like to play the Dutch way, but maybe
        I need to change...the only right way is
the winning way.'

Top 20 League Appearances

1	Alec McNair	1905-25	548
2	Paul McStay	1982-97	514
3	Billy McNeill	1959-75	486
4	Roy Aitken	1976-90	483
4	Packy Bonner	1978-95	483
6	Jimmy McMenemy	1903-20	458
7	Danny McGrain	1971-87	441
8	Patsy Gallagher	1912-26	434
9	Charlie Shaw	1913-25	421
10	Jimmy McStay	1923-34	409
11	Andy McAtee	1911-24	405
12	Willie McStay	1917-29	399
13	Alec Thomson	1923-34	391
13	Jim Young	1903-17	391
15	Bobby Evans	1947-60	385
16	Jimmy McGrory	1923-38	378
17	Adam McLean	1917-28	367
18	Peter Grant	1984-97	364
19	Tommy Burns	1975-90	356
20	Joe Dodds	1909-22	352

Above: Midfield maestro Paul McStay was forced to retire through injury in the summer of 1997.

League Cup Record 1968-97 – The Highs and Lows

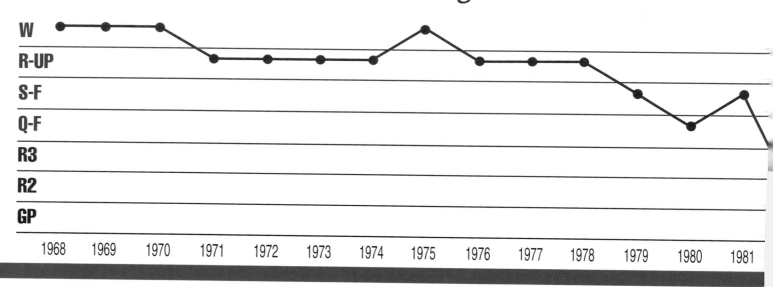

	W	R-UP	S-F	Q-F	R3	R2	GP

1968 1969 1970 1971 1972 1973 1974 1975 1976 1977 1978 1979 1980 1981

Top 20 League Scorers

1	Jimmy McGrory	1923-38	397
2	Jimmy Quinn	1901-15	191
3	Patsy Gallagher	1912-26	187
4	Bobby Lennox	1962-80	163
5	Steve Chalmers	1959-71	156
6	Jimmy McMenemy	1903-20	144
7	Adam McLean	1917-28	128
8	Sandy McMahon	1891-1903	126
9	Jimmy McColl	1914-20	117
10	John 'Yogi' Hughes	1961-72	116
11	Tommy McInally	1920-28	112
12	Kenny Dalglish	1969-77	111
13	Brian McClair	1984-87	99
14	Joe Cassidy	1913-24	94
15	John 'Dixie' Deans	1972-76	88
15	Alec Thomson	1923-34	88
15	Willie Wallace	1967-72	88
18	John Campbell	1891-1903	87
19	Charlie Nicholas	1979-83 & 1990-95	85
20	Jimmy Johnstone	1963-75	82
20	Charlie Napier	1930-35	82

Above: Brian McClair enjoyed four fruitful years at Parkhead before claiming further trophies in more than a decade with Manchester United.

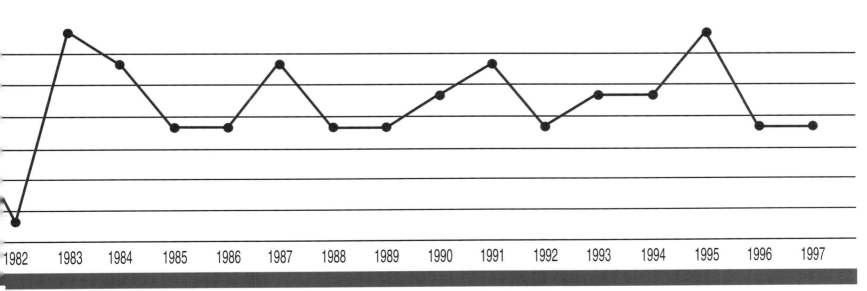

League Record 1968-97

DIVISION ONE					1980-81	1st	56	84-37
Season	Pos	Pts	F-A		1981-82	1st	55	79-33
1967-68	1st	63	106-24		1982-83	2nd	55	90-36
1968-69	1st	54	89-32		1983-84	2nd	50	80-41
1969-70	1st	57	96-33		1984-85	2nd	52	77-30
1970-71	1st	56	89-23		1985-86	1st	50	67-38
1971-72	1st	60	96-28		1986-87	2nd	63	90-41
1972-73	1st	57	93-28		1987-88	1st	72	79-23
1973-74	1st	53	82-27		1988-89	3rd	46	66-44
1974-75	3rd	45	81-41		1989-90	5th	34	37-37
					1990-91	3rd	41	52-38
PREMIER DIVISION					1991-92	3rd	62	88-42
Season	Pos	Pts	F-A		1992-93	3rd	60	68-41
1975-76	2nd	48	71-42		1993-94	4th	50	51-38
1976-77	1st	55	79-39		*Introduction of three points per win*			
1977-78	5th	36	63-54		1994-95	4th	51	39-33
1978-79	1st	48	61-37		1995-96	2nd	83	74-25
1979-80	2nd	47	61-38		1996-97	2nd	75	78-32

Left: The stars of 1970, from left,
Willie Wallace, Tommy Gemmell,
Bertie Auld and Billy McNeill.

FA Cup Record 1968-97 – The Highs and Lows

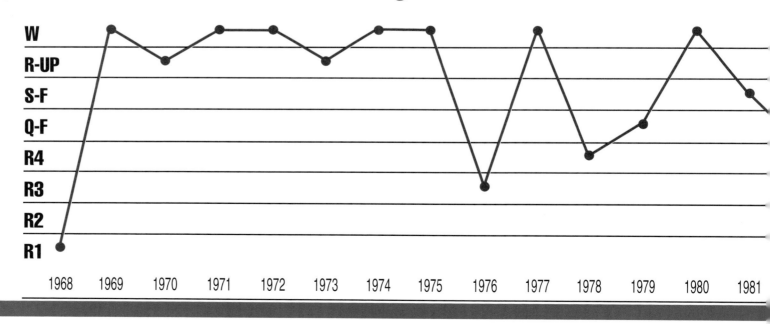

FA Cup Milestones 1968-97 *(see details of Highs & Lows below)*

Season	Opponents	Score	Season	Opponents	Score
1967-68	Dunfermline Athletic	0-2	1982-83	Aberdeen	0-1
1968-69	Rangers	4-0	1983-84	Aberdeen	1-2
1969-70	Aberdeen	1-3	1984-85	Dundee United	2-1
1970-71	Rangers	2-1	1985-86	Hibernian	3-4
1971-72	Hibernian	6-1	1986-87	Hearts	0-1
1972-73	Rangers	2-3	1987-88	Dundee United	2-1
1973-74	Dundee United	3-0	1988-89	Rangers	1-0
1974-75	Airdrie	3-1	1989-90	Aberdeen	0-0 (8-9 pens)
1975-76	Motherwell	2-3	1990-91	Motherwell	0-0, 2-4
1976-77	Rangers	1-0	1991-92	Rangers	0-1
1977-78	Kilmarnock	1-1, 0-1	1992-93	Falkirk	0-2
1978-79	Aberdeen	1-1, 1-2	1993-94	Motherwell	0-1
1979-80	Rangers	1-0	1994-95	Airdrie	1-0
1980-81	Dundee United	0-0, 2-3	1995-96	Rangers	1-2
1981-82	Aberdeen	0-1	1996-97	Falkirk	1-1, 0-1

Left: Roy Aitken's name went down in history as the player who captained Celtic to the Centenary Double.

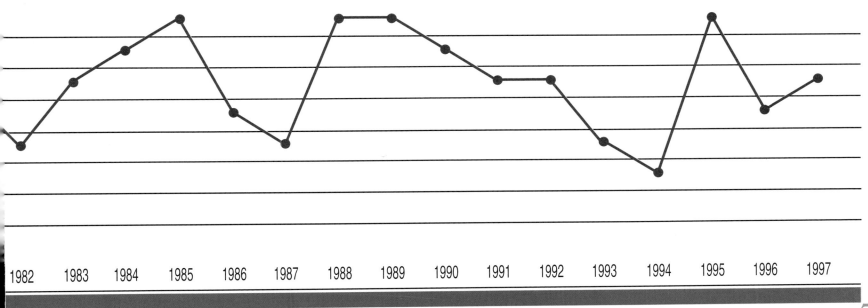

79

Honours

1888-89	FA Cup Runners-up	1955-56	FA Cup Runners-up
1891-92	Division One Runners-up and FA Cup Winners	1956-57	League Cup Winners
		1957-58	League Cup Winners
1892-93	Division One Champions and FA Cup Runners-up	1960-61	FA Cup Runners-up
		1962-63	FA Cup Runners-up
1893-94	Division One Champions and FA Cup Runners-up	1964-65	FA Cup Winners and League Cup Runners-up
1894-95	Division One Runners-up	1965-66	Division One Champions, FA Cup Runners-up and League Cup Winners
1895-96	Division One Champions		
1897-98	Division One Champions		
1898-99	FA Cup Winners	1966-67	Division One Champions, FA Cup Winners, League Cup Winners and European Cup Winners
1899-1900	Division One Runners-up and FA Cup Winners		
1900-01	Division One Runners-up and FA Cup Runners-up	1967-68	Division One Champions and League Cup Winners
1901-02	Division One Runners-up and FA Cup Runners-up	1968-69	Division One Champions, FA Cup Winners and League Cup Winners
1903-04	FA Cup Winners	1969-70	Division One Champions, FA Cup Runners-up, League Cup Winners and European Cup Runners-up
1904-05	Division One Champions		
1905-06	Division One Champions		
1906-07	Division One Champions and FA Cup Winners	1970-71	Division One Champions, FA Cup Winners and League Cup Runners-up
1907-08	Division One Champions and FA Cup Winners	1971-72	Division One Champions, FA Cup Winners and League Cup Runners-up
1908-09	Division One Champions	1972-73	Division One Champions, FA Cup Runners-up and League Cup Runners-up
1909-10	Division One Champions		
1910-11	FA Cup Winners		
1911-12	Division One Runners-up and FA Cup Winners	1973-74	Division One Champions, FA Cup Winners and League Cup Runners-up
1912-13	Division One Runners-up	1974-75	FA Cup Winners and League Cup Winners
1913-14	Division One Champions and FA Cup Winners	1975-76	Premier Division Runners-up and League Cup Runners-up
1914-15	Division One Champions		
1915-16	Division One Champions	1976-77	Premier Division Champions, FA Cup Winners and League Cup Runners-up
1916-17	Division One Champions		
1917-18	Division One Runners-up	1977-78	League Cup Runners-up
1918-19	Division One Champions	1978-79	Premier Division Champions
1919-20	Division One Runners-up	1979-80	Premier Division Runners-up and FA Cup Winners
1920-21	Division One Runners-up		
1921-22	Division One Champions	1980-81	Premier Division Champions
1922-23	FA Cup Winners	1981-82	Premier Division Champions
1924-25	FA Cup Winners	1982-83	Premier Division Runners-up and League Cup Winners
1925-26	Division One Champions and FA Cup Runners-up	1983-84	Premier Division Runners-up, FA Cup Runners-up and League Cup Runners-up
1926-27	FA Cup Winners		
1927-28	Division One Runners-up and FA Cup Runners-up	1984-85	Premier Division Runners-up and FA Cup Winners
1928-29	Division One Runners-up	1985-86	Premier Division Champions
1930-31	Division One Runners-up and FA Cup Winners	1986-87	Premier Division Runners-up and League Cup Runners-up
1932-33	FA Cup Winners	1987-88	Premier Division Champions and FA Cup Winners
1934-35	Division One Runners-up		
1935-36	Division One Champions	1988-89	FA Cup Winners
1936-37	FA Cup Winners	1989-90	FA Cup Runners-up
1937-38	Division One Champions	1990-91	League Cup Runners-up
1938-39	Division One Runners-up	1994-95	FA Cup Winners and League Cup Runners-up
1950-51	FA Cup Winners		
1953-54	Division One Champions and FA Cup Winners	1995-96	Premier Division Runners-up
1954-55	Division One Runners-up and FA Cup Runners-up	1996-97	Premier Division Runners-up

Above: Striker Tommy Johnson was brought from Aston Villa in early 1997 in an attempt to bring silverware back to Parkhead.